At Issue

The Federal Budget Deficit

Other Books in the At Issue Series:

At Issue

The Federal Budget Deficit

Susan Hunnicutt, Book Editor

GREENHAVEN PRESS
A part of Gale, Cengage Learning

GALE
CENGAGE Learning™

Detroit • New York • San Francisco • New Haven, Conn • Waterville, Maine • London

Christine Nasso, *Publisher*
Elizabeth Des Chenes, *Managing Editor*

© 2010 Greenhaven Press, a part of Gale, Cengage Learning.

Gale and Greenhaven Press are registered trademarks used herein under license.

For more information, contact:
Greenhaven Press
27500 Drake Rd.
Farmington Hills, MI 48331-3535
Or you can visit our Internet site at gale.cengage.com

For product information and technology assistance, contact us at

Gale Customer Support, 1-800-877-4253
For permission to use material from this text or product, submit all requests online at
www.cengage.com/permissions

Further permissions questions can be emailed to permissionrequest@cengage.com

Articles in Greenhaven Press anthologies are often edited for length to meet page requirements. In addition, original titles of these works are changed to clearly present the main thesis and to explicitly indicate the author's opinion. Every effort is made to ensure that Greenhaven Press accurately reflects the original intent of the authors. Every effort has been made to trace the owners of copyrighted material.

Cover photograph © Images.com/Corbis.

LIBRARY OF CONGRESS CATALOGING-IN-PUBLICATION DATA

The federal budget deficit / Susan Hunnicutt, book editor.
    p. cm. -- (At issue)
  Includes bibliographical references and index.
  ISBN 978-0-7377-4685-3 (hardcover) -- ISBN 978-0-7377-4686-0 (pbk.)
  1. Budget deficits--United States--Juvenile literature. 2. Government spending policy--United States--Juvenile literature. I. Hunnicutt, Susan.
  HJ2051.F389 2010
  339.5'230973--dc22
                                     2009041737

Printed in the United States of America
1 2 3 4 5 6 7 14 13 12 11 10

Contents

Introduction

In the summer of 2009, with the annual federal budget short-fall approaching $1.8 trillion and with the nation bending under nearly $13 trillion in accumulated indebtedness, the House of Representatives approved the Statutory Pay-As-You-Go Act of 2009 (also known as PAYGO). The bill was initiated by President Barack Obama in the early days of his administration and introduced in the House of Representatives by a group of fiscally conservative Democrats who were joined by the House majority leader and the director of the White House Office of Management and Budget (OMB). Fashioned by its broad base of Democratic supporters as a way to control future growth of the federal budget deficit, the bill required that new spending increases be paid for by corresponding spending cuts or tax increases. Likewise, future tax cuts would have to be offset by corresponding cuts in spending.

The Blue Dog Coalition, a key group of Democrats with a history of supporting balanced budget initiatives, characterized the Statutory Pay-As-You-Go Act of 2009 as an important step in getting Congress to reduce federal spending, and as an "enforcement tool" for getting the country on a path to fiscal responsibility. "We have fought tirelessly to rein in reckless federal spending and put an end to our spiraling deficit," Dennis Cardoza, a Democratic congressman from California who voted for the proposal, said in a 2009 article in the *Modesto Bee*.

Congressional Republicans did not support the Statutory Pay-As-You-Go Act of 2009. Instead they put forth a proposal of their own for controlling growth of the deficit by setting permanent caps on future spending while leaving future tax cuts unregulated. Paul Ryan, the Republican congressman from Wisconsin who introduced the alternative legislation, accused the Democrats of practicing "PR politics." Coming in the wake of an enormous stimulus plan and an equally enormous omnibus appropriations bill, the Pay-As-You-Go Act of 2009 was, he said in an National Public Radio interview, "kind of like buying a fire extinguisher after your house has burned down." Congressman Mike Pence, chairman of the House Republican Conference, expressed similar skepticism in a press release posted on the party's Web site (www.gop.gov): "Even under this PAYGO deal, discretionary spending—which amounts to 40 percent of all the spending—is being increased at 8 percent in this year and it's completely excluded from this. Emergency legislation, mandatory spending is not subjected. Hundreds of mandatory programs are not subjected. . . . The truth is when Democrats say PAYGO, they mean you pay and they go on spending."

House Democrats responded to criticism of their bill by pointing to the Budget Enforcement Act of 1990, PAYGO legislation passed by a Democratic Congress under the George H.W. Bush administration. In fact, that law reversed the growth in the federal deficit, leading to a four-year period at the turn of the millennium during which the federal government ran a surplus. House Republicans replied that both the Congress and recent presidents have a history of implementing PAYGO legislation and then finding multiple ways to avoid doing what it requires.

This controversy highlights some important characteristics of the current discussion in Washington about the federal budget deficit. First, the message about specific proposals to control the deficit can seem straightforward, but the details frequently are complex and difficult to sort out. Second, discussion of proposals to balance the budget can and usually do become highly politicized. Finally, in 2009 both the Blue Dog Democrats and the Republicans have generally pledged support for the idea of reducing the deficit by appealing to the idea of fiscal responsibility—in other words, it is irresponsible for lawmakers to allow the budget to go so far out of balance; it is responsible to take measures to reduce the deficit.

Stanley Collender, a communications professional, columnist, and author of the blog Capital Gains and Games, has questioned this way of thinking about how the government spends money. Collender, who has written and spoken regularly about the federal budget process for several years, argues that it is short-sighted to equate fiscal responsibility with pledges to reduce the deficit or balance the budget without paying close attention to how the money is being spent. "The president's budget is both a political statement and an accounting document," he wrote during the George W. Bush era, in a 2004 article in the *Jewish Daily Forward*. "It sets out the White House's priorities and agenda and tells us what they will cost."

For Collender, fiscal responsibility means making a plan, then working out the details of what it will cost and how it will be financed. It is important to consider spending in close connection to policy goals because the purpose of the budget is to equip the government to do the things that people expect it to do, including defending the country, ensuring that the food supply is safe, and supporting communities in the aftermath of unavoidable natural disasters, such as fires and hurricanes. "We want the federal government to do more than we are willing to pay for it to do," Collender said in an October 2007 post to his blog. He described the federal budget at that time as "a picture of under-funded accommodations" and argued that what was needed was a budget that demonstrated commitment to addressing a carefully selected list of priorities. When balancing the budget—or getting rid of the deficit—is the only issue being discussed, it seems people inevitably are disappointed with the way the government is performing.

As the varied points of view presented in this volume show, the budget deficit is a topic that evokes passionate conviction and intense disagreement. Just how serious is the current high level of deficit spending by the U.S. government? What are the causes of the imbalance? What would a responsible federal budget look like? Should the budget always be balanced, or are there other economic issues to be considered? How can lawmakers balance their responsibility to articulate a vision of prosperous and sustainable communities with the necessity of keeping government spending within prudent bounds? These are some of the questions considered in *At Issue: The Federal Budget Deficit.*

The United States Is Addicted to Deficit Spending

Liz Wolgemuth

Liz Wolgemuth writes for the Money & Business section of U.S. News & World Report.

Many economists on both the left and the right argue that a large federal budget deficit is necessary, for the near term, to slow or reverse economic recession. However, others believe that burgeoning deficits will suck money from the private sector, cause interest rates to rise, hurt the dollar, and damage the United States' credit rating. One way of breaking America's spending addiction is to rein in spending for entitlements, such as Medicare, Medicaid, and Social Security.

Anyone familiar with addiction knows when an intervention is long past due. So here goes: America, we care about you very much. You're the best. But some big changes need to be made, dude. You need to kick your out-of-control deficit spending habit. Will you please agree to seek treatment?

A recession may seem like a bad time to fret about government spending. Certainly, many economists argue that Uncle Sam needs to pour massive amounts of money into the economy to make up for plummeting spending and investment by consumers and businesses. But even if you fear we're on track for a depression, the upcoming budget shortfalls have to be alarming. The 2009 budget deficit will very likely be in the range of $2 trillion, according to Daniel Clifton, head of policy research at Strategas Research Partners. At nearly 14 percent of GDP [gross domestic product], that potential deficit figure would blow by the post–World War II high of 6 percent in 1983. It would also shatter the still-shocking $1.2 trillion estimate from the Congressional Budget Office [CBO], but that preliminary figure didn't include the crucial final tab of the stimulus package.

Headed for a Meltdown

This short-term budget shortfall comes courtesy of multitudinous money meltdowns and mishaps listed in the CBO's report. The agency projects a 6.6 percent drop in government revenues, thanks, in part, to an estimated $86 billion decline in individual income taxes and an $81 billion drop in corporate income taxes for fiscal year 2009. Other factors contributing to the red ink include the government's takeover of Fannie Mae and Freddie Mac [the Federal National Mortgage Association and the Federal Home Mortgage Corporation, respectively]; the bank bailout; beefed-up spending on unemployment benefits and food stamps; and—hanging like the sword of Damocles [an ancient Greek allusion that emphasizes the danger that comes with power]—the growing cost of funding Social Security, Medicare, and Medicaid. The three entitlements eat up an expanding portion of government expenditures—up from 16 percent 40 years ago to 40 percent today, according to a Treasury Department report. The long-term unfunded liabilities from Medicare and Social Security have been pegged at about $99 trillion by Richard W. Fisher, president of the Federal Reserve Bank of Dallas. "Unless we take steps to deal with it, the long-term fiscal situation of the federal government will be unimaginably more devastating to our economic prosperity than the subprime debacle and the recent debauching of credit markets that we are now working so hard to correct," Fisher said in a 2008 speech aptly titled "Storms on the Horizon."

Budget deficits have long been a controversial issue in Washington. Democrats hammered President [Ronald] Reagan and Republicans over big deficits in the 1980s and pointed with pride to the budget surpluses under President [Bill] Clinton. The issue flared again under the [George W.] Bush administration when government books again started hemorrhaging. (It didn't help when former Vice President Dick Cheney was said to have matter-of-factly declared that "deficits don't matter.")

But thanks to the recession, being deep in the red [in debt] is the new black [showing a surplus]. Many economists, on the left and right, insist that running up this short-term debt is necessary to keep the recession from becoming a depression. It could even help the long-term growth potential of the economy if some of the spending is directed to investments in education, energy, and infrastructure.

Social Security reform still seems to be political kryptonite, given the Bush administration's lack of success when it tried to fix the system.

Martin Feldstein, the conservative Harvard economist and former Reagan adviser, has made headlines by endorsing government stimulus spending as a way of boosting the economy. "Spending would directly add to production and employment. Temporary tax cuts are likely to be saved and not added to spending," Feldstein says. Liberal economist and Nobel Prize winner Paul Krugman can hardly get enough stimulus. Krugman has been calling for government to pick up spending where consumers have, en masse, left off—and he's repeatedly opined that the [Barack] Obama administration's plans may not be large enough.

Voters Do Not Pay Much Attention

Voters have rarely cared much about deficits. Perhaps the only recent exception was in 1992, when presidential candidate Ross Perot harped on the issue and snagged nearly 20 percent of the popular vote. The lack of interest isn't surprising. The average voter knows the deficit hangover won't be his or her headache to treat, and seniors have gotten jumpy when legislators talk entitlements. Social Security reform still seems to be political kryptonite, given the Bush administration's lack of success when it tried to fix the system.

Some economists are less blasé about the ballooning deficit. Arthur Laffer, the Reagan-era tax-cut guru famous for the Laffer Curve, is one of the holdouts. Trillion-dollar deficits would be "disastrous for the economy," Laffer says. Free-market stalwarts like Laffer argue that the private sector spends money more efficiently and productively than government. And borrowed money will eventually have to be paid for through higher taxes that will take money from the private sector. Indeed, some of the biggest tax increases of the past generation—1982, 1990, 1993—came at times of concern over high budget deficits.

Investors seem to be showing an increased concern about the U.S. government's ability to shoulder its debt payments.

This binge-spending hangover could hurt in other ways, too—and not just when the kiddos grow up and face higher taxes to pay for both today's spending orgy and tomorrow's entitlement spendathon. The vast increase in public debt could yank interest rates higher, damage the value of the dollar, dampen private-sector investment and innovation (by trapping so many investor dollars in treasuries), and even tarnish the nation's pristine credit rating.

It's hard to imagine this country without a perfect credit score, but in a recent report affirming the country's AAA debt rating, Standard & Poor's credit analysts noted rising risk to the nation's credit profile from the slowing economy and fast-growing budget shortfalls.

The national debt is now $10.6 trillion, nearly double what it was a decade ago and 73.6 percent of GDP. That rising total could cause trouble in a couple of ways. For starters, there is the possibility that international investors will lose their previously voracious appetite for U.S. treasuries. David Walker, the former head of the Government Accountability Office who is now president of the Peter G. Peterson Foundation, says he thinks one of the greatest risks is posed by the country's overreliance on foreign lenders, the biggest of which are China, Japan, and Britain. "Half our debt today is held by foreign lenders, and 70 to 80 percent of the new debt is being purchased by foreign lenders primarily because they have savings and we don't," Walker says. "In the short term, we're lucky they're willing to do that because it provides us with capital and attractive interest rates. But it's not prudent for us to rely upon that over time."

Will Investors Get Nervous?

The United States has, for the most part, had few problems finding willing investors. But with massive amounts of debt in the market, paying investors back could get seriously pricey when the economy stabilizes, says Andrew Busch, global currency strategist for BMO Capital Markets in Chicago. He notes that the CBO estimates that interest rates on three-month treasuries will jump from 0.2 percent in 2009 to 4.7 percent in 2013. "You're laying the groundwork for serious problems down the road," Busch says. Rising interest rates could slow an embryonic economic recovery.

Investors seem to be showing an increased concern about the U.S. government's ability to shoulder its debt payments.

The cost of buying insurance against government defaults has been climbing over the past several months: According to CMA [Credit Market Analysis] DataVision, prices on five-year credit default swaps rocketed to 74.9 basis points toward the end of January [2009] (meaning investors were forking over $74,900 annually to protect $10 million worth of treasuries). Credit default swaps on U.S. debt were trading at 6 basis points as recently as April 2008.

One way to reassure investors that today's spending binge marks the end of an era of fiscal recklessness is by doing something about entitlements. Some solutions are pretty well known: raising the retirement age, boosting the limit on income subject to the Social Security tax (now at $106,800), and indexing benefits to inflation rather than wages. Medicare reform solutions include lower payments to providers and higher payroll taxes. Many have called for a bipartisan congressional committee to overhaul the budget process. None of the solutions . . . will be pretty or painless. But dealing with hangovers rarely is.

2

The Iraq War and the Tax Cuts Created the Federal Budget Deficit

Steven Leser

Steven Leser, a Democratic Party activist, is an editor for OpEd-News. He writes about politics, science, and health.

The Iraq war has cost the United States $487 billion, or $130 billion every year since it began. The George W. Bush administration's tax cuts removed $1.35 trillion from government revenues between 2002 and 2007. These two choices are the most important ingredients in a witches' brew of poor choices that have created the current economic crisis. The most effective way to restore financial health would be to end the war and reverse the Bush tax cuts.

A s we head into this horrific stagflation economy that I described in my January 18, [2008] article "Stagflation Returning to the US Economy after 30 Years," and even predicted . . . in [my] article, "Election 2006 Continued Wrap Up—The Coming Economic Swoon . . . ," I think most people are probably wondering "How did we get here?" It is hard to imagine that we find ourselves in such a bad situation. A severe economic downturn coupled with high inflation and a massive budget deficit, less than eight years after the end of the [President Bill] Clinton era that ushered in balanced budgets and a booming economy. Where did we go wrong?

When an economy goes bad, there is usually no single reason why. While there are several mistakes that the [George W.] Bush administration made that brought us to this point, there are two actions/issues under the administration's control to which we can point and say, without those, we would not be here. Those acts are the Iraq war and the Bush tax cuts.

Nearly five years of war in Iraq has thus far [in January 2008] cost the United States economy $487 Billion dollars. If you include the amounts appropriated through 2008, the amount goes to almost $620 Billion dollars. This averages out to a yearly cost of the Iraq war of nearly $130 Billion per year. In 2006, the entire US Gross Domestic Product [GDP] was $13 Trillion dollars. That means that expenditures on the Iraq war totaled 1% of the US' Gross Domestic Product every year since its inception. Put another way, one out of every $100 dollars spent in the US economy for the past five years has been on the Iraq war. What one has to keep in mind is that this is money that would ordinarily not have been spent on anything. That means 1% more dollars are circulating as a result of the Iraq war and that by itself is very inflationary. If you want another frightening statistic, the entire World Gross Product in 2006 was approximately $48 trillion dollars. So for every $400 spent worldwide, $1 of it was spent by the US on the Iraq war. I'm not sure anything personifies waste more than that statistic.

We can also look at the Iraq war expenditures as measured against the total amount taken in and spent by the government. The 2007 total budget expenditures were $2.8 trillion dollars. Not counted in this total were supplemental expenditures of which the Iraq war expenditures are examples. The approximately $125 Billion dollars spent on Iraq in 2007 represents almost 5% of total Government spending last year [2007]. Since total government income was $2.4 Trillion dollars giving us a budget deficit of $400 Billion dollars, we can say that the Iraq war expenditures represent an amount equal to approximately 30% of all deficit spending.

A Witches' Brew of Bad Choices

If we also add the Bush tax cuts, some of which have been in effect since 2001, some since 2003, we have the final ingredients of the witches' brew that caused our current crisis. We all should have known what was coming since we were warned. In February of 2003, over 450 of the finest economic minds in the country including *ten* individuals who had been awarded the Nobel Prize for Economics, issued a statement calling the 2003 Bush tax cut plan "misdirected." The statement read in part:

> Passing these tax cuts will worsen the long-term budget outlook, adding to the nation's projected chronic deficits. This fiscal deterioration will reduce the capacity of the government to finance Social Security and Medicare benefits as well as investments in schools, health, infrastructure, and basic research. Moreover, the proposed tax cuts will generate further inequalities in after-tax income.

> To be effective, a stimulus plan should rely on immediate but temporary spending and tax measures to expand demand, and it should also rely on immediate but temporary incentives for investment. Such a stimulus plan would spur growth and jobs in the short term without exacerbating the long-term budget outlook.

The best thing that could be done for the US economy right now would be for us to bring an immediate end to the Iraq war.

One has to note that the 2003 tax cuts to which the economists were objecting were in addition to those passed in 2001, which cut $1.35 Trillion dollars from government revenues for the past six years. The 2003 tax cuts were described by Wikipedia and the Congressional Budget Office as causing an additional $340 Billion loss in government revenues. Most of that tax cut money went to the wealthiest Americans who spent a lot of that money on expensive foreign goods or invested a sizeable amount of that money in foreign markets. If you are reviewing the numbers, you can see that without the Bush tax cuts, we would still have a balanced budget, even including the ill conceived Iraq war.

If Bush had never engineered the tax cuts he put into place over the first three years of his tenure, and he had not fought the Iraq war, we would have a federal budget that had a several hundred billion dollar surplus. We would have a lot less government spending and a lot less money in circulation, meaning lower prices and less inflationary pressure. If, in 2001 and 2003, Bush had listened to the consensus of the best economic minds in the country and instead of tax cuts had enacted temporary demand-side stimulus packages, lower and middle income Americans would have had the money they needed to ride out the recession but the government would have not had the loss of $1.7 Trillion in revenue over the last six years. You can talk about the housing bubble and subprime mortgages and the lending crisis, but without the loss of $1.7 trillion dollars in revenue and without the expenditures of $600 Billion on the Iraq war, I feel confident in saying we could have dealt with those issues.

Ending the War Would Yield Giant Savings

The best thing that could be done for the US economy right now would be for us to bring an immediate end to the Iraq war. That would mean $130 Billion dollars that would not need to be spent this year and $130 Billion that would not need to be spent in 2009. We could use that $260 Billion and provide relief to those who are or will become unemployed, or we could hold onto it and partially close the gap between government income and expenditures. We can further boost government revenues and have money available to help those who need it by bringing an end to the Bush tax cuts. But we have to be careful. If we give too much demand side assistance, we will create additional inflation. The actions by the Fed [Federal Reserve] to lower interest rates and the upcoming bipartisan stimulus package are incorrect knee-jerk reactions to much bigger and more complex problems. As I wrote in my "Stagflation" article of January 18, these responses by the Fed and the government stimulus package are the wrong things to do if we are in a stagflation economy. We will see a temporary weakening, but slightly positive response in GDP and the financial markets accompanied by rising inflation. This positive response will last less than six months after which the economy will swoon again even more severely with a continued rise in prices. Inflation is the big problem right now, not the negative GDP growth and not the loss of jobs. If we don't deal with inflation, the GDP and jobs will suffer greater and greater problems until we do.

Bush and the Republicans need to be held responsible for their failed policies. If you start an expensive war for reasons other than those that you told the public and you have a massive, bankrupting tax giveaway for the rich and these policies lead to economic ruin, you should have to pay some sort of price. At the very least, that price should be a loss of the White house for the GOP [Republican party] and a Democratic super-majority in both houses of congress.

3

The Federal Budget Deficit Is the Result of Unruly Entitlement Spending

Alison Acosta Fraser

Alison Acosta Fraser is director of the Thomas A. Roe Institute for Economic Policy Studies at the Heritage Foundation.

Federal spending will top 15 percent of America's gross domestic product (GDP) in 2009, and the deficit is projected to reach $1.2 trillion, even before a stimulus bill is passed. A large part of the deficit is the result of entitlement spending for programs such as Social Security, Medicare, and Medicaid. The president and responsible law-makers need to put long-term obligations for these programs at the center of the budget process, develop a package of reforms to make them affordable, establish policies to assess spending changes, and, ultimately, to create a long-term budget framework for entitlement spending. If this issue is not addressed, the president's stimulus legislation will create a sea of red ink and debt.

Congress and President-elect Barack Obama have set their sights on a massive economic stimulus bill crammed full of spending projects intended to "jolt" the economy into recovery. By some counts this package may reach $1 trillion, or nearly 85 percent of the total of all budget bills passed last year [2008].

This is not the way to spur economic recovery. Even Obama recognizes he faces a difficult challenge: how to keep

Alison Acosta Fraser, "Any Stimulus Legislation Must Include Budget Reforms to Address Long-Term Challenges," Heritage Foundation Web Memo, January 9, 2009. Copyright © 2009 The Heritage Foundation. Reproduced by permission.

the stimulus focused on short-term deficit spending and avoid a huge, long-term expansion of the federal government—and with it a dramatic increase in the staggeringly large unfunded obligations due mainly to Social Security, Medicare, and Medicaid. To deal with that challenge, Obama should work with fiscally responsible Members of Congress to include four key budget reforms in any stimulus legislation:

1. Put long-term obligations from Social Security, Medicare, and Medicaid front and center in the budget process;

2. Establish a bipartisan congressional commission to develop a package of long-term reforms for entitlements;

3. Establish equitable policies for assessing and enforcing spending and revenue changes in the budget; and

4. Create a long-term budget for entitlement spending.

Spending and Deficits Hit New Records

Federal spending is projected to top 25 percent of GDP [gross domestic product] in 2009, according to the Congressional Budget Office (CBO), the highest it has been since World War II, and that is *before* any stimulus legislation. The deficit is projected to reach $1.2 trillion by the end of this year [2009], and any stimulus would likely push the deficit to more than $1.6 trillion.

Similar large deficits are projected to continue into the future. Such deficits are a loud alarm to which policymakers must listen: Federal spending is out of control. But even they ignore the deeper fiscal problems of Social Security and Medicare. These programs together, not even counting Medicaid, have an unfunded obligation that is equivalent to a mortgage of $43 trillion. Future generations will be forced to pay for those obligations through higher taxes unless the programs are modernized.

Budget Restraint Is Necessary

While making the case for his massive short-term stimulus proposal, President-elect Obama acknowledged the threat entitlements pose to the economy, noting, "If we do nothing, then we will continue to see red ink as far as the eye can see." He called budget reform "an absolute necessity," and he has pledged to confront the problems from Social Security and Medicare in his budget.

Budget writers in Congress are also alarmed. Senate Budget Committee Chairman Kent Conrad (D-ND), called the deficit "jaw dropping," and House Budget Committee Chairman Jack Spratt (D-SC) was suffering "sticker shock." They and their ranking member counterparts have encouraged lawmakers to tackle the long-term budget problems posed by these entitlement programs. Conrad and Senator Judd Gregg (R-NH) have urged Congress to link the stimulus with action to address the long-term budget crisis.

Entitlement spending grows on auto-pilot, in conjunction with the programs' regulatory framework, so there is not an open or transparent consideration of priorities or budgetary trade-offs.

If President-elect Obama is serious about fiscal responsibility, he and responsible Members of Congress must insist on budget reforms to prevent further deterioration of an already alarming long-term budget problem and require action to tackle these challenges directly. To that end, he and responsible lawmakers should insist on these four key budget reform measures being included in any stimulus package:

Four Key Reforms Are Needed

1. Put long-term obligations from Social Security, Medicare, and Medicaid front and center in the budget process, with an up-or-down vote on any budget that will increase debts on future gen-

erations. Such a measure could easily be incorporated into the annual budget resolution. This would provide a more accurate and transparent assessment of the federal government's commitments and provide all Americans with a vivid picture of the problem. All major policy changes should be scored over the long term to indicate what impact they would have on the total unfunded obligations of the government. That would provide lawmakers and the public with a better understanding of the true long-term costs of new legislation. And to put Members on record on their attitude to burdening our children and grandchildren, they should have to vote during the annual budget process if the proposed budget will increase long-term obligations.

2. Enact a bipartisan congressional commission to develop a package of long-term reforms that will make these programs affordable. Bipartisan legislation to implement this type of commission was introduced in the previous Congress: the SAFE Act (H.R. 3654), co-sponsored by Representatives Jim Cooper (D-TN) and Frank Wolf (R-VA), and the Bipartisan Task Force for Responsible Fiscal Action Act (S 2063), co-sponsored by Conrad and Gregg. Under both bills, a commission would craft detailed recommendations for a fast-track vote in Congress. The SAFE Act would have the added advantage of a two-step process. Its first phase would be a series of nationwide public hearings to talk frankly about the long-term fiscal problem and the tough options for fixing it and to build public support for congressional action on a broad plan of action.

3. Establish equitable policies for assessing and enforcing spending and revenue changes in the budget. Any budget enforcement mechanism is based on changes in projected spending and revenues. The CBO projects a spending baseline by assuming that all the laws authorizing spending—such as the highway or farm programs, or even appropriations—will be extended year after year and spending levels will continue even if they expire regularly under existing law. But when it comes to taxes, the CBO's baseline is current statute, and any rates reductions, deductions, credits, etc., that are scheduled to expire are assumed to do so. The lopsided result is that spending is given a free ride under the baseline while any reduction in the growth of taxes is assumed to be temporary.

This skewed baseline means current "PAYGO" [so-called pay as you go] rules are biased toward tax increases. Thus, for any enforcement mechanism to be considered fair and to be effective, it must be based on the same baseline treatment for both spending and revenues. Indeed, Obama's own advisors have already criticized this lopsided policy treatment, which stacks the deck in favor of higher spending and higher taxes.

4. Create a long-term budget for entitlement spending. Unlike "discretionary" programs such as defense and education, "mandatory" entitlement programs like Medicare and Social Security are not budgeted annually. Entitlement spending grows on auto-pilot, in conjunction with the programs' regulatory framework, so there is not an open or transparent consideration of priorities or budgetary trade-offs. And since spending levels are simply the product of individuals using their entitlement, there is in a sense no budget—just a projection of likely total costs. And as they grow unchecked, these entitlements crowd out other programs and priorities.

With the first baby boomers recently retiring, America is experiencing the first waves of the entitlement tsunami.

This must change, by constraining entitlement programs with a real budget. To be sure, retirement programs require longer time horizons and planning than typical discretionary programs so that beneficiaries will not face unexpected annual changes in benefits. Therefore, Congress should create a long-term framework for a constrained entitlement budget that would be periodically evaluated to ensure that these programs are sustainable and affordable over the long term. This could be done by creating a long-term budget window—for example, 30 years. All spending would be reviewed every five years, and the commission could recommend measures for Congress to ensure that the programs live within this budget framework.

It Is Time to Tackle Entitlements

There are many reasons to be concerned over the unprecedented stimulus spending now being proposed, including the ineffectiveness of Keynesian [an economic theory, based on the ideas of British economist John Maynard Keynes, that encourages low interest rates and increased government spending to stimulate the economy] pump priming, the perils of such an immense hike in government spending, and the creation of new permanent government programs. With the first baby boomers recently retiring, America is experiencing the first waves of the entitlement tsunami. The stimulus legislation could set the stage for a permanent sea of red ink and an even larger tsunami of debt. Substantive budget reforms are needed to prevent such a scenario from occurring.

Since President-elect Obama is intent on signing a massive spending bill, he must insist that it does not result in huge permanent government programs and thus potentially trillions of dollars in new burdens on our children and grandchildren. He must demonstrate his commitment to tackle the long-term entitlement challenges by working with Members of Congress to build sound budget process reform measures into the stimulus legislation. If he does not do so, the young Americans who voted for him should question how serious he is about protecting their financial future.

4

Deficits Do Not Matter

Joe Conason

Joe Conason is a columnist for Salon *and the* New York Observer. *He is also the author of a book,* It Can Happen Here: Authoritarian Peril in the Age of Bush.

Republicans frequently demand "fiscal responsibility," but they have a repeated history of spending trillions of dollars at the same time that they are passing tax cuts, thereby increasing the size of the deficit. The truth is that large budget deficits—for example, the one that was created during World War II—do not necessarily damage the economy. If large deficits are incurred for the sake of worthwhile goals, the economy can benefit.

[F]ormer vice president] Dick Cheney once observed that "deficits don't matter," which may well have been the most honest phrase he ever uttered. His words were at least partly true, which is more than can be said for the great majority of the vice president's remarks—and they certainly expressed the candid attitude of Republicans whenever they attain power. His pithy fiscal slogan should remind us that much of the current political furor over deficit spending in the [President Barack] Obama budget is wrong, hypocritical, and worthy of the deepest skepticism.

In our time, the Republican Party has compiled an impressive history of talking about fiscal responsibility while running up unrivaled deficits and debt. Of the roughly $11 trillion in federal debt accumulated to date, more than 90 percent can be attributed to the tenure of three presidents: Ronald Reagan, who used to complain constantly about runaway spending; George Herbert Walker Bush, reputed to be one of those old-fashioned green-eyeshade Republicans; and his spendthrift son George "Dubya" Bush, whose trillion-dollar war and irresponsible tax cuts accounted for nearly half the entire burden. Only Bill Clinton temporarily reversed the trend with surpluses and started to pay down the debt (by raising rates on the wealthiest taxpayers).

Republicans in Congress likewise demanded balanced budgets in their propaganda (as featured in the 1993 Contract with America), but then proceeded to despoil the Treasury with useless spending and tax cuts for those who needed them least. Even John McCain, once a principled critic of those tax cuts, turned hypocrite when he endorsed them while continuing to denounce the deficits they had caused.

As history warns, there are things much worse than deficits and debt. One such thing was the Great Depression.

Deficit Spending Not So Bad After All

But was Cheney wrong when he airily dismissed the importance of deficits? In the full quotation, as first recounted by Paul O'Neill, Bush's fired Treasury Secretary, he said, "You know, Paul, Reagan proved deficits don't matter. We won the [Congressional] midterms [in November 2002]. This is our due." What he evidently meant—aside from claiming the spoils—was that the effects of deficit spending tend to be less dire than predicted. And that insight deserves to be considered if only because all the partisan barking over the projected deficits in the Obama budget is so hysterical—as if nothing could be worse than more federal spending.

Such is the institutional bias of the Washington press corps, which habitually refers to deficits "exploding" and to the nation "engulfed in red ink," and so on. But in fact the United States has recovered from considerably deeper indebtedness than that now on the horizon. Besides, as history warns, there are things much worse than deficits and debt. One such thing was the Great Depression, prolonged when Franklin Roosevelt decided to curb the deficits that had revived the economy, and ended only when he raised spending even higher in wartime. Another was worldwide fascist domination, a threat defeated by expanding America's public debt to unprecedented levels during World War II. No sane person cared then that public debt had risen well above gross domestic product.

Those scary charts and graphs often deployed to illustrate our parlous state of indebtedness rarely date back as far as the Forties and Fifties—and the reason is simple. The massive deficits incurred during the war didn't matter, as Cheney might say, because the wartime national investments in industry, technology and science undergirded a postwar boom that lasted for nearly three decades, creating the largest and most prosperous middle class in human history.

As Clinton proved in confronting the huge legacy of debt left over from the Reagan era, it is possible to raise taxes and slow spending without damage to the broader economy.

Where the Money Is Spent Matters

The average annual growth rate remained close to four percent for that entire period—and over time the combination of constant growth and smaller deficits reduced the ratio of debt to a fraction of its postwar dimension. What mattered more than the size of the deficits was whether they were spent on things that enabled consistent growth.

Today, President Obama is more troubled by the enormous threats to the nation's future than by deficits, even if they are projected in trillions of dollars. Clearly he believes that there are still some things worse than debt.

One such thing would be a global depression that drags on for several years. Another would be the catastrophic consequences of unchecked climate change, potentially more devastating than a world war; deteriorating public schools that will undermine democracy and demote us to secondary status; and a national health system that costs too much, provides too little care, and burdens enterprise. By investing now, he hopes to prevent disaster and create the conditions for sustainable expansion.

Not all of the warnings about deficit spending are false. Wasteful federal spending can eventually lead to inflation; excessive deficits can cause interest rates to rise, although that doesn't always occur. But as Clinton proved in confronting the huge legacy of debt left over from the Reagan era, it is possible to raise taxes and slow spending without damage to the broader economy.

As for the Republicans, it is difficult to listen to their doomsaying predictions without laughing. They want us to worry about the evils of deficit spending when they obviously don't worry about that at all. Just yesterday [March 26, 2009], the House Republican leadership distributed what they called an alternative budget. Missing from that thin sheaf of papers was any attempt to estimate what their plan would cost and how much it would increase the deficit. Their ironic ignorance of history was illustrated by their single concrete proposal. They insist that we must cut the maximum tax rate from 36 percent to 25 percent—or the same as the top rate in 1929, on the eve of the Great Depression.

5

Democrats and Republicans Often Change Their Opinions About Deficits

Veronique de Rugy

Veronique de Rugy is a senior research fellow at the Mercatus Center at George Mason University. Her research interests include the federal budget, tax competition, and financial privacy issues.

The Democratic and Republican parties both have a history of reversing their opinions about deficits—at times opposing deficit spending to block certain programs and supporting such spending at other times to pay for programs they support. Some economists argue that deficit spending is a drain on the economy, driving up the cost of credit by increasing the demand for capital. However, this has not been conclusively proven. Whether or not it is true that deficit spending leads to higher interest rates, it is clear that lower spending results in smaller government. Opposing deficit spending is one way of keeping government small.

On January 5, *The New York Times* reported that "the incoming Democratic chairmen of the House and Senate Budget Committees today called upon the President to work with them on a deficit-reducing package that would include tax increases and spending cuts." Concerned that deficit pro-

Veronique de Rugy, "When Do Deficits Matter? While Democrats and Republicans Switch Sides, Economists Try to Pin Down a Tipping Point," *Reason*, vol. 41, May 2009, pp. 21–22. Copyright © 2009 by Reason Foundation, 3415 S. Sepulveda Blvd., Suite 400, Los Angeles, CA 90034. www.reason.com. Reproduced by permission.

jections were unrealistic because they didn't include military costs, Democrats urged the administration to increase taxes on the wealthiest Americans.

That was January 5, 1987. Ronald Reagan was president, and the deficit had reached almost 5.4 percent of gross domestic product (GDP). Now, three decades later, Democrats have changed their minds about the dangers of deficit spending. In February 2009, the nonpartisan Congressional Budget Office estimated that the deficit will reach $1.2 trillion this year—roughly 8.3 percent of GDP. That giant increase is attributable mainly to Washington's September 2008 bank bailout and the federal takeover of mortgage lenders Fannie Mae and Freddie Mac.

When President George W. Bush turned a massive surplus into a series of giant deficits, few in the [Republican Party] objected.

And that figure assumes that the 2009 budget issued last year [2008] by the [George W.] Bush administration will stay at its proposed level, which it surely won't. The calculation does not include the cost of the Iraq and Afghanistan wars, and it doesn't include the chunk of the new $787 billion stimulus bill that will be spent in 2009. Add all these numbers together, and the deficit swells to $2 trillion, or roughly 13.5 percent of GDP.

The Biggest Deficits Since World War II

This is by far the highest share of the economy that deficits have taken up since World War II. It is well over twice the record set by Ronald Reagan in the 1980s. Yet we don't see Democrats denouncing the deficit explosion on the network news, like they did two decades ago.

The Democrats aren't the only ones who have reversed their opinions about deficits. Republicans were relatively comfortable with Reagan's unbalanced budgets. And when President George W. Bush turned a massive surplus into a series of giant deficits, few in the GOP [Republican Party] objected. During the administration's internal debates over proposed tax cuts in 2002, Vice President Dick Cheney reportedly told Treasury Secretary Paul O'Neill that "Reagan proved deficits don't matter."

In a 2007 interview with *Fortune*, Cheney refined his position, explaining that "you've got to evaluate them relative to other priorities. Another priority, for example, would be defending the nation in wartime."

In other words, if the spending that creates deficits supports your party's programs, fiscal irresponsibility doesn't matter. Republicans don't mind deficit spending if the trade-off is tax cuts and more money for the military. Democrats tolerate deficits when they buy goodies for union workers and allow other increases in domestic outlays.

Even Economists Do Not Agree

But can you blame politicians for flip-flopping on the issue? Economists—even free market ones—can't agree on whether deficits matter either.

The main academic debate over deficit spending is whether it raises long-term interest rates and therefore reduces economic growth. Some economists believe that deficits financed by borrowing increase the demand for capital. This in turn increases the price of capital—i.e., interest rates. Higher interest rates then increase the cost of doing business, which slows down the economy.

Others disagree. In 1987, for instance, the Harvard economist Robert Barro wrote in his textbook *Macroeconomics* that "this belief does not have evidence to support it." When deficits get bigger, he argued, individuals increase their savings to offset government spending.

Even without assuming Barro's private savings offset, scholars haven't been able to find a clear correlation between interest rates and deficit spending. In 1993, for instance, the North Carolina State University economist John Seater surveyed the academic studies on deficits and interest rates. After reviewing the literature, Seater concluded that the data "are inconsistent with the traditional view that government debt is positively related to interest rates."

[Consider] 30-year mortgage rates, inflation rates, and deficits as a percentage of GDP during the last three decades. Although the federal budget deficit both rose and fell during this period, the 30-year mortgage rate has trended consistently downward.

Still, most free market economists are more cautious about denying a correlation exists. Arnold Kling, an adjunct scholar with the Cato Institute who blogs at *EconLog*, argues that the reason we haven't seen a correlation between budget deficits and interest rates so far is that foreign investment in American assets has increased over the years, dulling the impact of fiscal policy. The real question—and the real threat—is what will happen if that investment stops, or even if it merely slows down.

At What Point Does It Matter?

Moreover, deficits have reached a level that economists haven't really studied before. Current circumstances remind Kling of "a guy jumping out of a building from the 10th floor, passing the third floor, and saying, 'It's all fine so far.'" Deficits do not matter up to a certain point. But at which level do we hit the ground with a splat? Ten percent of GDP? Twenty percent?

Economic debates aside, deficits certainly do matter if you care about shrinking the size of the state. Budget gaps are a kind of Ponzi scheme [a fraudulent investment system that pays investors with other investments, rather than with profit]. Any year the federal government spends more money than it collects in tax revenue, we have a budget deficit. That means the citizens through their taxes authorize politicians to spend a certain amount yet the government spends more.

The plan is to pay this additional spending back with future taxes, just as Bernard Madoff [a businessman arrested in December 2008] figured he'd pay off early investors with dollars from pigeons [i.e., gullible people] he conned down the road. As with any Ponzi scheme, there will inevitably come a time when the con is exposed, along with all the participants' losses.

John Maynard Keynes, the 20th century's preeminent defender of deficit spending, famously quipped, "In the long run, we are all dead." Keynes did not give much guidance, though, on how we would pay for the funeral.

6

Liberals Should Care About Reducing the Federal Budget Deficit

Andrew L. Yarrow

Andrew L. Yarrow is vice president and Washington director of Public Agenda, a nonpartisan think tank. He is the author of Forgive Us Our Debts: The Intergenerational Dangers of Fiscal Irresponsibility.

Contrary to political stereotypes, the Democratic Bill Clinton administration reduced deficit spending and practiced fiscal restraint, while the Republican George W. Bush administration that followed it increased spending, cut revenues, and expanded the federal debt. Nevertheless, many liberals are suspicious of the idea of reforming America's spend-and-tax policies. Liberals should care about deficits because of the debt that gets passed on to their children, because of the higher likelihood of future economic crises as deficits erode economic well-being, and in order to preserve future spending choices.

From Ronald Reagan until Robert Rubin [secretary of the treasury under Bill Clinton], fiscal restraint, deficit reduction, and "balancing the budget" were all but exclusively the province of conservatives. In practice, the last decade or so has changed that political equation, as President Clinton and Treasury Secretary Rubin successfully cut spending, raised revenues, and balanced the federal budget for the first time since

Andrew L. Yarrow, "Why Liberals Should Care About Deficits," *Balitmore Sun*, September 21, 2008. Copyright © 2008 Baltimore Sun. Reproduced by permission of the author.

the 1960s—only for President [George W.] Bush to increase spending, cut revenues, and increase federal debt by more than $4 trillion. Of course, in both cases, a Republican-controlled Congress helped.

Suspicious of Reduction Proposals

Yet, despite this seemingly startling reversal in which party could best claim the mantle of fiscal responsibility, many liberals remain deeply suspicious of—if not downright hostile to—ideas of reforming America's spend-and-tax policies that have left us $9.6 trillion in the hole, with another $50 trillion in long-term unfunded liabilities. Although there is increasing lip-service, and some action, about bipartisanship in getting the United States to balance its out-of-whack books, many liberals fail to see why fiscal responsibility is in their interests—as well as in the interests of conservatives and all Americans.

With mandatory spending, for entitlements and growing debt service, eating two-thirds of federal spending . . . little will be left for anything else.

So, why should liberals care? Why shouldn't they just see debt and deficit reduction as conservative Trojan horses to cut social programs and attack government? And why should they "give in" on programs like Social Security when a Republican administration has plunged the nation $4 trillion deeper into debt?

There are at least three major reasons.

But, first, a few basic myths need to be dispelled: 1) ending the Bush tax cuts alone won't solve the problem; 2) ending the Iraq war or making other defense cuts won't solve the problem; and 3) we can't keep Social Security, Medicare, and Medicaid as they are without hurting millions of other equally deserving Americans.

A key reason that liberals, like all Americans, should care about fiscal responsibility comes down to what the philosopher John Rawls calls "intergenerational justice." By running up ever greater debt, we pass trillions of dollars of IOUs to our children and grandchildren. They will have to pay the bills that we have run up—in higher taxes, reduced benefits, slower economic growth, and, possibly, economic Armageddon. Would you take your 3-year-old son or granddaughter to buy a new house and hand him or her the mortgage? If liberals believe in equity, providing equal (or better opportunities) for future generations as for today's Americans is just as important as creating a more just and equitable society in the present.

A second reason for liberal concern should flow from a commitment to economic security for all. The potential consequences of inaction include either economic crises of various flavors or the slow erosion of Americans' economic well-being. Whether growing debt spooks markets and sends the economy into a maelstrom or "simply" makes it harder for either business or government to raise funds to invest in people and create good jobs, future generations' living standards are threatened—something presumably of concern across the political spectrum. And it's always the poor and middle class who suffer most.

Finally, there are the sheer mathematical realities of what our out-of-kilter federal finances are doing, and will do, to the kinds of initiatives that liberals love. With mandatory spending, for entitlements and growing debt service, eating two-thirds of federal spending (a proportion that is rising), little will be left for anything else. Domestic discretionary spending—the catch-all for education, science, transportation, energy, environment, justice, and so much else—gets just one-sixth of the federal budget. Defense accounts for one-fifth.

National Priorities Will Be Tested

On present trajectories, without massive increases in taxes, all that (including defense) gets squeezed out by out-of-control mandatory spending over the next generation. So, no more money to improve children's education or health. Nothing left to help Americans afford homes or get skills for good jobs. Nada for development of new energy sources or any other scientific research. Forget the environment or rebuilding our crumbling infrastructure. And, of course, nothing for the kinds of beneficial new initiatives that Americans have creatively, and often even wisely, developed throughout our history.

Federal spending is a gauge of national priorities. If we let debt continue to grow, we'll be saying, in effect, that our priorities are to fund nothing more than well-intentioned, but now unaffordable, entitlement programs, and to consume public resources now at the expense of future generations. This is not a call to jettison Social Security, Medicare, and Medicaid—which have made so many Americans' lives better—but to radically reform them so that the United States can fund efforts to address so many other national needs.

If making our country and our children's lives better isn't a liberal (and conservative, and American) agenda—what is?

7

Conservatives Are Using the Deficit to Attack Medicare and Social Security

Robert Kuttner

Robert Kuttner is a coeditor of the American Prospect *and a senior fellow at Demos, a public policy group. He is the author of* Obama's Challenge: America's Economic Crisis and the Power of a Transformative Presidency.

Fiscal conservatives are using the budget deficit to attack "unfunded liabilities"—such as Social Security, Medicare, and Medicaid—which, they say, will burden our children with debt. Their plan is to impose caps on programs, such as Social Security and Medicare, to offset trillion-dollar deficits. The reality, however, is that America is already underfunding important investments, including childcare, college tuition, and health insurance. The attack on social insurance is an ideological assault disguised as fiscal restraint. Debt needs to increase now to support economic growth, then gradually be reduced once the economy has recovered.

With the enactment of a large economic stimulus package, fiscal conservatives are using the temporary deficit increase to attack a perennial target—Social Security and Medicare. The private-equity investor Peter G. Peterson, who launched a billion-dollar foundation last year [2008] to warn that America faces $56.4 trillion in "unfunded liabilities," is a

Robert Kuttner, "The Deficit Hawks' Attack on Our Entitlements," *Washington Post*, February 23, 2009, p. A19. Reproduced by permission of the author.

case in point. Supposedly, these costs will depress economic growth and crowd out other needed outlays, such as investments in the young. The remedy: big cuts in programs for the elderly.

The Peterson Foundation is joined by leading "blue dog" (anti-deficit) Democrats such as House Budget Committee Chairman John Spratt of South Carolina and his counterpart in the Senate, Kent Conrad of North Dakota. The deficit hawks are promoting a "grand bargain" in which a bipartisan commission enacts spending caps on social insurance as the offset for current deficits.

President [Barack] Obama's economic advisers devised . . . [a recent] White House fiscal responsibility summit to signal that the president takes the deficit seriously and to lay the groundwork for such a bipartisan deal. Originally, Peterson was slated to be a featured speaker.

But Capitol Hill sources say that Democratic congressional leaders were skeptical of the strategy. The summit has been reduced to a lower-profile, half-day event; Peterson will attend but no longer has top billing, and Obama reportedly is lukewarm about the idea of a commission.

Even without a raise for working America, Social Security needs only minor adjustments.

Obama should indeed be wary of such a plan, and official briefings on his first budget suggest that he will drastically reduce the deficit by 2013, but without going after social insurance.

What's wrong with the story of entitlements wrecking the economy? Plenty.

The Deficit Hawks Are Wrong

For starters, the $56 trillion "unfunded liability" figure relies on creative accounting. Only about $6.36 trillion is the actual public debt, according to the U.S. Treasury. Most of the number Peterson cites is a combination of the 75-year worst-case projections for Social Security, Medicare, and Medicaid.

These three programs face very different challenges and remedies. Social Security's accounts are actually near long-term balance. The Congressional Budget Office puts the 75-year shortfall at only about one-third of 1 percent of projected gross domestic product [GDP].

Social Security is financed by taxes on wages—and since the mid-1970s, wage growth has stagnated. If median wages rose with productivity growth, as they did during the first three decades after World War II, Social Security would enjoy a big surplus. Even without a raise for working America, Social Security needs only minor adjustments.

Medicare really does face big deficits. But that's because Medicare is part of a hugely inefficient, fragmented health insurance system. It makes no sense to "reform" Medicare in isolation.

Today's young adults are already falling out of the middle class because of the high costs of the investments we don't adequately finance socially—child care, college tuition, and health insurance.

If we just cap Medicare, needy seniors would get bare-bones care while more affluent people could supplement their insurance out of pocket. The decent cure for Medicare's cost inflation lies in comprehensive universal health insurance so that the entire system is more efficient and less prone to inflation. You don't hear many budget hawks supporting that brand of reform.

The deficit hawks' story also contends that we are sacrificing our children's future by too much (deficit) spending on the elderly. In fact, today's young adults are already falling out of the middle class because of the high costs of the investments we don't adequately finance socially—child care, college tuition, and health insurance. But fiscal conservatives seldom call for increased investment in the young. Today's young, of course, will be tomorrow's retirees, and they will need social insurance, too.

The overall bottom line? The economy we bequeath to our children has everything to do with getting growth back on track and almost nothing to do with imagined future deficits.

History provides a parallel. At the end of World War II, the public debt was about 120 percent of GDP—about three times today's ratio. Yet the heavily indebted wartime economy stimulated a quarter-century postwar boom—because all that debt went to recapitalize American industry, advance science and technology, retrain our unemployed, and put them to work.

We need to increase public spending and debt now to restore economic growth and then gradually reduce the debt ratio once recovery comes. Social Security has little to do with this challenge. Nor does Medicare, if we reform our overall health system.

Since the early 1980s, Peter G. Peterson has been warning that future entitlement deficits would crash the economy. Yet when the crash came, the cause was not deficits but wild speculation on Wall Street.

Now, with 401(k) plans swooning and health benefits being cut, Social Security and Medicare are the two bedrock programs that keep tens of millions of elderly Americans from destitution. Why perversely cut these programs to pay for the sins of Wall Street? The attack on social insurance is really an ideological assault, dressed up as fiscal high-mindedness.

8

Massive Budget Deficits Will Burden Our Children with Debt

Mike Crapo

Senator Mike Crapo, a Republican from Idaho, is a member of the Senate Banking, Housing, and Urban Affairs Committee.

Deficits have reached staggering proportions, and the 2010 budget will leave an appalling legacy of debt for our children and grandchildren. It will increase discretionary spending by almost $600 billion and mandatory spending by $1.1 trillion over ten years. In addition, the administration's claim that 95 percent of people will not be affected by tax increases is disingenuous, because several of the proposed taxes, such as the "cap and trade" energy tax, will eventually be passed on to consumers. Future entitlement spending amounts to two-thirds of all spending in the budget. Young people understand the need for fiscal restraint, and so should Congress.

Recently, Idaho high school students came to Washington and brought a petition signed by 400 fellow students calling for a balanced budget. I am glad that teens are showing concern and being proactive about what is happening in our economy and the actions (or inactions) of Congress and the administration. This petition shows foresight—the president's [President Barack Obama's] fiscal 2010 budget is scheduled to further indebt these students, their children and even their grandchildren.

Mike Crapo, "Obama Budget Stains Children with Red Ink," *The Hill*, March 24, 2009. Copyright © 2009 Capitol Hill Publishing Corp. Reproduced by permission.

A Troubling Legacy for Young People

However, it's troubling that these young people, who are just embarking on the journey of adulthood, rich in promises of education, job opportunities and a family, have to worry about the egregious and irresponsible behavior of those a generation ahead. What an appalling legacy for us to leave them. As a member of the Senate Budget Committee, I am convinced that Congress must not use the president's budget request as a reliable budget guideline.

A proposed brand-new tax on energy, couched in the term "cap and trade," will impose new taxes of up to $2 trillion on . . . electrical, gasoline, and natural gas, to name a few.

According to the non-partisan Congressional Budget Office (CBO), the president's budget request contains outlays in fiscal 2009 alone of $4 trillion and a deficit of $1.8 trillion. Any claim about cutting the deficit in half in a few years is nonsense when considered in the current budget context—sort of like "slashing prices" by 50 percent the day after you've doubled them. (In January 2009, before the American Recovery and Reinvestment Act of 2009 and the fiscal 2009 appropriations omnibus were passed, CBO predicted a budget deficit of $703 billion for fiscal 2010. The current budget deficit for fiscal 2010 is projected to be approximately $1.4 trillion.) Additionally, any decreases in the deficit are temporary: Estimates in a decade project $5.1 trillion in outlays and a deficit still well over $1 trillion. The budget also includes an estimated tax increase of at least $1.8 trillion over 10 years. Those students who came to see me in March will be six years out of college, paying higher taxes and bearing a financial burden in which they played no part in creating or making a decision about.

The budget increases discretionary spending by almost $600 billion and increases mandatory spending by $1.1 trillion over 10 years—increases because these amounts do not include what is slated to be spent under current law. Finally, CBO's baseline deficit of $1.8 trillion for fiscal 2009, which does include Troubled Asset Relief Program I (TARP I), the 2009 omnibus and the stimulus, does not account for the money spent under TARP II.

On the tax increases: The administration claims that tax increases will not affect 95 percent of taxpayers. This number is only accurate when looking at income tax. No matter what language you choose to use, revenue collected for the federal treasury is still tax. A number of taxes in the proposed budget will raise revenue by increasing the cost of doing business. Those costs, in turn, will be passed on to consumers in the form of higher prices for goods and/or services. It's disingenuous to pretend otherwise. For example, a proposed brand-new tax on energy, couched in the term "cap and trade," will impose new taxes of up to $2 trillion on carbon-emitting entities—electrical, gasoline, and natural gas, to name a few. These costs will end up in household energy bills and transportation fuel expenditures.

On spending: This budget's mandatory spending—Medicare, Medicaid, Social Security, and interest on the national debt—amounts to about two-thirds of all spending in the budget. The rest, discretionary, is divided between the half that is allocated to national defense and homeland security and the other half directed to non-defense discretionary spending. This budget significantly grows our government in non-defense programs, and cloaks an actual reduction in defense spending by projecting spending for Iraq that is counter to the administration's stated policy.

The Numbers Are Frightening

Finally, public debt numbers are positively frightening. The numbers at the end of 2008 showed this portion of the debt to be $5.8 trillion. With the spending implemented and proposed over the past six months, the debt held by the public will double in five years and triple in 10. The wall of debt is growing; the response: more taxes and zero spending restraints (except, dangerously, the military). During a recent Senate Budget Committee hearing, Treasury Secretary Timothy Geithner said taxes would have a "chilling" effect on the economy at a time when we need to be getting the economy going again. However, he defended the expiration of the tax cuts in 2011 as happening when they anticipate the economy to be better. I asked the secretary at that time if the tax increases were contingent on a strong economy. He ducked the question, which says to me that taxes are scheduled to increase regardless of the state of the economy.

What Congress and now the administration has imposed on American families over the past six months spends too much, taxes too much, and borrows too much. High school students understand this; so should Congress! We need fiscal restraint in the form of responsible spending and tax policy, designed to reduce expenditures and refrain from unnecessarily penalizing the very sector of our economy in which the seeds of growth are found—small businesses. Instead, what we are faced with is unrestrained fiscal behavior in the form of irresponsible tax policy that includes massive spending and unchecked entitlement growth, and which utterly ignores debt. In New York City's Times Square, the National Debt Clock is expected to be redesigned this year to accommodate $10 trillion. That many one-dollar bills lined up end-to-end would stretch to the moon and back at least 2,000 times. It's time to take a step back and really evaluate what this means for our country's future.

9

Focus on the Deficit Distracts Attention from Real Economic Problems

Dean Baker

Dean Baker is codirector of the Center for Economic and Policy Research.

The economy is in a meltdown, with more than a hundred thousand homes a month being foreclosed on, almost seven hundred thousand job losses a month, default rates on credit cards at record levels, and major banks insolvent. In this environment it does not make sense to focus on record deficits. The government's first priority has to be to address the economic crisis. If policy makers can return us to a period of strong economic growth, the deficit problem eventually will be resolved.

In the movie *Lars and the Real Girl*, the main character imagines that a female blow-up doll is his fiancé. To humor Lars, his brother and sister-in-law go along with the charade. Over the course of the movie, more people are drawn into the circle, until eventually the whole town is treating Bianca the blow-up doll as one of its leading citizens.

This seems to pretty well describe the debate over the budget deficit, except it's not clear that many people realize it's a charade. The main story is that Lars' budget hawk counterparts are upset that the deficits projected for 2013 or 2019 are

Dean Baker, "Budget Deficits and Blow Up Dolls: It's the Economy, Stupid!" *Huffington Post*, March 25, 2009. Copyright © 2009 HuffingtonPost.com. Reproduced by permission of the author.

too large. They want President [Barack] Obama to commit to spending cuts and/or tax increases in order to bring these deficits to levels they consider acceptable.

The unreality of this picture is striking because the budget hawks seem not to notice that we are in the middle of an economic meltdown.

Economic Meltdown Is Biggest Threat

People are losing their homes through foreclosures at the rate of more than 100,000 a month. The default rates on credit cards, car loans, and other debt is at record levels. Most of our major banks are effectively insolvent.

It is especially annoying to hear the whining from . . . deficit hawks since their whining in prior years helped to drown out serious discussion of the dangers posed by an $8 trillion housing bubble.

Home and stock prices have plummeted, destroying most of the wealth of the baby boom cohort as they stand on the edge of retirement. The economy is shedding almost 700,000 jobs a month, with the unemployment rate rapidly approaching the highest level since the Great Depression.

In this context we are supposed to be up in arms over the deficit projections for 2013 or 2019? This is a bit like someone complaining about the lawn not being mowed at a time when the house is on fire; it's just not the first priority. And the media all seem to go along with the charade—yes, they are very concerned about the projected deficit for 2013, just as the characters in the movie expressed concern about the health of Bianca the blow-up doll.

It is especially annoying to hear the whining from this group of deficit hawks since their whining in prior years helped to drown out serious discussion of the dangers posed by an $8 trillion housing bubble. While some of us were yelling at the top of our lungs about the imminent disaster that would hit the economy when the housing bubble burst, the media chose to focus on these deficit hawks with their dire warnings about budget deficits 40 or 50 years in the future.

Because the media and political elites chose to pay more attention to the deficit hawks than those warning about the housing bubble, we now get to enjoy the current economic crisis. And, one result of the economic crisis is (drum roll, please) . . . record deficits.

To put the point so simply that even a *Washington Post* editor can understand it: because the media highlighted the views of the people who were ranting about the deficit rather than the views of people who understood the economy, we both got a wrecked economy and larger deficits.

The moral to this story is that the economy must take priority, not only because the state of the economy is what most directly determines people's well-being, but also because the state of the economy will be the most important determinant of the deficit.

The experience of the 1990s provides an example of exactly this sort of story. In January of 1994 the Congressional Budget Office projected that the deficit in 1999 would be $204 billion or 2.4 percent of GDP [gross domestic product]. This projection incorporated the impact of President [Bill] Clinton's tax increase and spending cuts.

It turned out that there was a surplus of $125 billion in 1999, or 1.4 percent of GDP. This shift from deficit to surplus of 3.8 percentage points of GDP (equivalent to $540 billion in 2009) was not caused by further spending cuts or tax increases; it was caused by the strong economic growth of the period.

There is no guarantee that President Obama's policies will be successful in restoring strong growth, but they are clearly a step in the right direction. If we have strong growth, then our deficits will be manageable. If the economy remains weak, the deficit will remain a serious burden no matter how much we raise taxes or cut spending.

Someone has to tell the deficit hawks that their blow-up doll is not real. The issue is the economy, not the deficit.

10

Carefully Planned Deficit Spending Can Lead to a Stronger Economy

Robert H. Frank

Robert H. Frank is an economist at Cornell University and a visiting faculty member at the Stern School of Business at New York University.

The consensus among economists is that short-term deficits can help end recessions and that whether long-term deficits matter depends on how borrowed money is spent. The current deficit is not too large. In fact, it may not be large enough to revive the economy.

Are you confused about whether large federal budget deficits matter?

No wonder, when disagreement about deficits is popping up everywhere. Even among Republicans, there is no unity on this basic issue. Defending his recent proposal to freeze government spending, Representative John A. Bochner, the House minority leader, said, "We simply cannot afford to mortgage our children and grandchildren's future to pay for this big government spending spree." But Martin Feldstein, the Harvard economist, disagrees. An adviser to the past three Republican presidents, Professor Feldstein warns that failure to run large deficits would prolong the current economic downturn.

Because important policy decisions hinge on whether deficits matter, this is an opportune moment to take stock of what we know. The good news is that there is little disagreement among economists who have studied the issue. The consensus is that short-run deficits help end recessions, and that whether long-run deficits matter depends entirely on how government spends the borrowed money. If failure to borrow meant forgoing productive investments, bigger long-run deficits would actually be better than smaller ones.

In 1929, President Herbert Hoover thought that the best response to a collapsing economy was to balance the federal budget. With incomes and tax receipts falling sharply, that meant cutting federal spending. But as almost all economists now recognize, President Hoover was profoundly mistaken.

A Downward Spiral

When a downturn throws people out of work, they spend less, causing still others to be thrown out of work, and so on, in a downward spiral. Failure to use short-run deficits to stimulate spending amplifies that spiral, causing further declines in tax receipts and even bigger deficits. That this path makes no sense is a settled issue.

But what about long-run deficits? To think more clearly about them, we must recognize that carrying debt is costly. The government can pay just the interest on its debt each year, or it can pay interest plus some additional amount to reduce the principal. The yearly payment is clearly greater in the second case, just as a homeowner's monthly payment is larger with a 10-year mortgage than with a 30-year one. But the total burden of the various repayment options (in technical terms, their "present value") is exactly the same. It's a simple trade-off between intensity of burden and duration of burden.

No matter which option we choose, money spent to service debt can't be spent for other things we value. But that doesn't mean we should always borrow less. The main issue is what we do with the borrowed money.

If we simply use the money to buy bigger houses and cars, deficits make us unambiguously worse off in the long run. That's why the explosive increase in the national debt during the [George W.] Bush administration was a grave misstep.

Trillions of dollars, many of them borrowed from China, financed tax cuts for the wealthy, who spent much of their added wealth on things like bigger mansions. But beyond a certain point, when everyone builds bigger, the primary effect is merely to raise the bar that defines the size of home that people feel they need. Much of the interest we'll pay on debt incurred during the Bush years is thus money down the drain.

Borrowing Can Make Us Stronger

In contrast, borrowing for well-chosen investments doesn't make us poorer. Road maintenance is a case in point. Failure to repair roads in a timely way could mean eventually spending two to four times as much for the work. Even ignoring the fact that timely repairs would reduce the substantial vehicle damage from potholes, it would be much cheaper to borrow the money and do maintenance on schedule.

Once the downturn ends, there should be no need to incur additional debt.

It's also useful to put the nation's debt burden into perspective. Over the last eight years [during the Bush presidency], Bush administration deficits raised the national debt by almost $5 trillion. Given the current crisis, it's easy to imagine a similar increase during the next four years. At recent interest rates, servicing $10 trillion of extra debt costs about $400 billion annually—a big amount, to be sure, but less than 3 percent of the economy's full-employment output. We'll still be the richest country on the planet even after paying all that interest.

Once the downturn ends, there should be no need to incur additional debt. Indeed, there are many ways to pay down debt without requiring painful sacrifices. A $2 tax on each gallon of gasoline, for example, would generate more than $100 billion in additional revenue a year. Europeans, who pay more than $2 a gallon in gasoline taxes, have adapted by choosing more efficient cars—and they appear no less satisfied with them.

We could also levy a progressive consumption surtax, which would not only generate additional revenue to pay down debt or finance additional public investment, but would also stimulate private savings by diverting money from those over-the-top coming-of-age parties that the wealthy stage for their children.

Notwithstanding the neo-Hooverite talk from stimulus-program opponents, the current deficit isn't too large. If anything, it may need to be even larger to revive the economy. In the long run, new sources of tax revenue could keep deficits from growing and could even pay down existing debt. But if the political system cannot figure out how to pay for productive investments with tax revenue, we'd still end up richer, on balance, by making those investments with borrowed money.

11

The Stimulus Bill Will Increase the Federal Deficit Yet Not Fix the Economy

Charles E. Grassley

Republican Charles E. Grassley is the senior U.S. senator from Ohio. He was the chairman of the Senate Finance Committee during the George W. Bush administration and is currently the committee's ranking member.

The stimulus bill is based on the theory that consumption drives the economy and that if you put money into the hands of consumers, they will spend the economy back to prosperity. According to this theory, the deficit does not matter. However, the only way government can put money into someone's hands is to take it from someone else. It is impossible to place a value on what might have been created if money had not been taken from one person and given to another. The stimulus bill will create a huge fiscal deficit that will be a drag on the economy. It is a very expensive way to create jobs, and it will not solve America's fiscal problems.

Our nation's fiscal outlook is grim. The Congressional Budget Office [CBO] projects the federal budget deficit will exceed $1 trillion this year [2009]. Despite this enormous deficit, President [Barack] Obama is urging Congress to enact a massive stimulus plan that would add another $1 trillion in government debt over the next ten years. The President and his advisors insist we must spend this money as quickly as possible in order to save our economy.

Charles E. Grassley, "A $1 Trillion Stimulus? Let's Look Before We Leap," U.S. Senate Floor Statement, February 4, 2009.

In normal times, such fiscal excess would be widely criticized and promptly rejected. But these are not normal times. We are told our economy faces the worst recession since the Great Depression. While such comparisons may be overblown, everyone is understandably concerned about the present state of our economy. Congress needs to take action to address declining growth and rising unemployment. But, we must not let our desire for a quick fix undermine our ability to address the real challenges we face.

A sustainable fiscal policy depends on a growing economy; and a sound economy depends on a sound fiscal policy. Unfortunately, there does not seem to be any consensus on what constitutes sound policy.

Spending Versus Saving

There are two opposing views on the economy. Some people say consumption is the key to economic growth. When people go shopping, the economy is good. According to this view, we need to spend more. Other people say investment is the key. When businesses invest, the economy is good. According to this view, we need to save more.

Some economists try to reconcile these opposing views by suggesting the correct view depends on the circumstances. When workers are fully employed and factories are fully utilized, they say we need to save more and increase supply. But, when workers are unemployed and factories are idled, they say we need to spend more and increase demand. While this explanation is appealing, it does not withstand careful scrutiny.

We are told that in order to stimulate the economy, all the government has to do is put money into the hands of consumers and they will spend us back into prosperity. The problem with this approach is that the only way the government can put money in someone's hands is by taking it from someone else's pockets—either in the form of taxes or borrowing.

This is a zero sum game in which one person's loss is another person's gain. Some economists try to obscure this fact by introducing a concept known as the marginal propensity to consume. That's a fancy way of saying some people spend more of their money than others.

According to this concept, low-income people are more likely to spend an extra dollar than high-income people. Thus, taking money from the rich and giving it to the poor will stimulate consumer demand and boost the overall economy.

Of course, the critics say this is not always true. During a recession banks are less willing to lend and businesses are less willing to borrow. Thus, some of the money previously available in the economy is no longer being used. It has been stuffed under the proverbial mattress, so to speak. Thus, advocates of fiscal stimulus claim the government can borrow and spend during a recession without crowding-out other private sector spending.

This is true only in the narrow sense that increasing the money supply allows the government to borrow and spend without reducing the amount of money available to others. But, in that sense this is really an argument about monetary policy masquerading as fiscal policy. Moreover, when the government borrows money, whether it is new money or old money, what the government is really borrowing is the resources it acquires. Thus, every dollar the government spends has an opportunity cost in terms of the potential alternative uses of those resources.

The Multiplier Effect on Our Cash

Much of the confusion over this point comes from the failure to recognize the nature of money in our economy. Economists often talk about the multiplier effect in order to explain how each dollar of government spending can result in more than a dollar of economic activity.

But, the multiplier effect is simply a way of illustrating the fact that if I give you a dollar, you will spend part of it and save part of it. The portion you spend goes to someone, who spends a portion and saves a portion, and so on, and so on. . . . Thus, one dollar effectively multiplies into many dollars.

Contrary to what some people might have you believe, the multiplier effect applies to every dollar, not just those spent by the government. According to Federal Reserve data over the past 50 years the ratio between our Gross Domestic Product [GDP] and our money supply—defined as currency plus bank reserves—has ranged from 10-to-1 to 20-to-1. In other words, every dollar in our economy supports between ten and twenty dollars of economic activity.

During a recession, there are fewer workers producing fewer goods and services. That is why it is called a recession. Because the level of output is lower, the level of spending is lower as well. That means the available dollars are being used less. Economists often refer to this as a decline in the velocity of money.

When the government borrows money for some activity that is what is seen. But what is not seen is what could have been created had those workers and resources been used in some other way.

The money no longer being used reflects the goods and services no longer being produced. With fewer goods and services available to buy, government efforts to borrow and spend will increase the money supply. Instead of the Federal Reserve increasing bank reserves to boost private lending, the government will increase borrowing to boost private spending. But, this is really monetary policy disguised as fiscal policy.

The success or failure of this policy will depend on how the additional money is used. Unfortunately, when some advocates of government stimulus talk about priming the pump, they give the impression that we can grow our economy by simply spending money, and it doesn't matter how we spend it.

Consider the following comments from [twentieth-century British economist] John Maynard Keynes:

"If the Treasury were to fill old bottles with banknotes, bury them at suitable depths in disused coal mines ... and leave it to private enterprise ... to dig the notes up again ... there need be no more unemployment."

Misguided Policies, Long-Term Disadvantages

Nearly everyone would recognize the ill effects of printing up $1 trillion and dropping it from helicopters. But, what if the government hired ten million Americans to dig holes and fill them back up, and paid them each $100,000? Would this prime the pump, and get our economy moving again? The answer should be obvious—it would be a complete waste of resources.

The 19th century economist Fredrick Bastiat once observed, "There is only one difference between a bad economist and a good one: the bad economist confines himself to the visible effect; the good economist takes into account both the effect that can be seen and those effects that must be foreseen."

When the government borrows money for some activity that is what is seen. But what is not seen is what could have been created had those workers and resources been used in some other way. The benefit of a government stimulus plan must be weighted against the cost. So far, there has been no comprehensive cost-benefit analysis of the proposed stimulus bill. This is a glaring omission given the recent comments that have been made by President Obama.

Shortly before his inauguration, President Obama gave a series of speeches and interviews. I would like to read a couple of sentences from them.

According to the January 16th [2009] *Washington Post*:

Obama repeated his assurance that there is 'near-unanimity' among economists that government spending will help restore jobs in the short term, adding that some estimates of necessary stimulus now reach $1.3 trillion.

"The theory behind it is I set the tone," Obama said. "If the tone I set is that we bring as much intellectual firepower to a problem, that people act respectfully towards each other, that disagreements are fully aired, and that we make decisions based on facts and evidence as opposed to ideology, that people will adapt to that culture and we'll be able to move together effectively as a team."

He added: "I have a pretty good track record at doing that."

In his January 10th radio address, President-elect Obama said:

Our first job is to put people back to work and get our economy working again. This is an extraordinary challenge, which is why I've taken the extraordinary step of working—even before I take office—with my economic team and leaders of both parties on an American Recovery and Reinvestment Plan that will call for major investments to revive our economy, create jobs, and lay a solid foundation for future growth.

I asked my nominee for chair of the Council of Economic Advisers, Dr. Christina Romer, and the vice president-elect's chief economic adviser, Dr. Jared Bernstein, to conduct a rigorous analysis of this plan and come up with projections of how many jobs it will create—and what kind of jobs they will be. . . .

The report confirms that our plan will likely save or create 3 to 4 million jobs. . . .

The jobs we create will be in businesses large and small across a wide range of industries. And they'll be the kind of jobs that don't just put people to work in the short term, but position our economy to lead the world in the long-term.

The jobs being created by the House bill could cost as much as 2.5 times more than jobs created without the stimulus bill.

These comments from President Obama are noteworthy for several reasons. First, he suggests a level of unanimity among economists that does not exist. Second, he suggests his Administration will make decisions based on the facts, instead of ideology. Third, he suggests his plan will create jobs that are more than just temporary.

The Surprising Costs of Job Creation

In that regard, I would note that the Congressional Budget Office released an analysis of the House stimulus bill. According to CBO, the House stimulus bill will create between 3 million and 8 million new jobs over the next three years, depending on whether the multiplier assumption is "Low" or "High."

Given the cost of the House bill, these figures imply a very surprising, and a very troubling, result. The CBO estimate shows that it will cost between $90,000 and $250,000 per job created.

These numbers should be contrasted to those under the CBO baseline which show GDP per worker is about $100,000.

In other words, the jobs being created by the House bill could cost as much as 2.5 times more than the jobs created without the stimulus bill. There's been a lot talk about "bang for the buck" around here. But, there doesn't seem to be any interest in actually making sure it happens. Before we spend another $1 trillion, we ought to make sure we are getting our money's worth.

It should also be noted that CBO's analysis only covers 2009 through 2011. But, if you assume the ratio of employment to government spending remains the same throughout the 10-year projection period, there will be only a few thousand new jobs. Moreover, if you adopt the standard assumption that increasing the national debt by $1 trillion will crowd out private sector investment, the net result will be fewer jobs because of the stimulus bill.

I have written a letter to the CBO Director requesting an analysis of both the House and the Senate stimulus bills. This analysis will cover the full 10-year period consistent with the January baseline. . . .

Again, let me repeat what I said at the beginning. Congress needs to take action to address declining growth and rising unemployment. But, before we spend another $1 trillion, Congress must take the time to look before we leap.

12

Cutting Military Spending Would Reduce the Federal Budget Deficit

Barney Frank

Barney Frank represents the Fourth District of Massachusetts in Congress and is chairman of the House Financial Services Committee.

The best way to reduce the budget deficit is to cut military spending. This would not hurt national security, because our military force is already overfunded. Even with substantial reductions in military spending, we would still be much stronger militarily than any combination of nations with whom we might be engaged. If we fail to cut military spending, it will be impossible to fund domestic spending at necessary levels.

I am a great believer in freedom of expression and am proud of those times when I have been one of a few members of Congress to oppose censorship. I still hold close to an absolutist position, but I have been tempted recently to make an exception, not by banning speech but by requiring it. I would be very happy if there was some way to make it a misdemeanor for people to talk about reducing the budget deficit without including a recommendation that we substantially cut military spending.

Sadly, self-described centrist and even liberal organizations often talk about the need to curtail deficits by cutting Social

Barney Frank, "Cut the Military Budget—II," *The Nation*, February 11, 2009. Copyright © 2009 by The Nation Magazine/The Nation Company, Inc. Reproduced by permission.

Security, Medicare, Medicaid, and other programs that have a benign social purpose, but they fail to talk about one area where substantial budget reductions would have the doubly beneficial effect of cutting the deficit and diminishing expenditures that often do more harm than good. Obviously people should be concerned about the $700 billion Congress voted for this past fall [2008] to deal with the credit crisis. But even if none of that money were to be paid back—and most of it will be—it would involve a smaller drain on taxpayer dollars than the Iraq War will have cost us by the time it is concluded, and it is roughly equivalent to the $651 billion we will spend on all defense in this fiscal year [2009].

Funds for War but Not Healthcare

When I am challenged by people—not all of them conservative—who tell me that they agree, for example, that we should enact comprehensive universal healthcare but wonder how to pay for it, my answer is that I do not know immediately where to get the funding but I know whom I should ask. I was in Congress on September 10, 2001, and I know there was no money in the budget at that time for a war in Iraq. So my answer is that I will go to the people who found the money for that war and ask them if they could find some for healthcare.

If . . . we were to cut military spending by 25 percent from its projected levels, we would still be immeasurably stronger than any combination of nations with whom we might be engaged.

It is particularly inexplicable that so many self-styled moderates ignore the extraordinary increase in military spending. After all, George W. Bush himself has acknowledged its importance. As the December 20 *Wall Street Journal* notes, "The president remains adamant his budget troubles were the result of a ramp-up in defense spending." Bush then ends this rare burst of intellectual honesty by blaming all this "ramp-up" on the need to fight the war in Iraq.

Current plans call for us not only to spend hundreds of billions more in Iraq but to continue to spend even more over the next few years producing new weapons that might have been useful against the Soviet Union. Many of these weapons are technological marvels, but they have a central flaw: no conceivable enemy. It ought to be a requirement in spending all this money for a weapon that there be some need for it. In some cases we are developing weapons—in part because of nothing more than momentum—that lack not only a current military need but even a plausible use in any foreseeable future.

It is possible to debate how strong America should be militarily in relation to the rest of the world. But that is not a debate that needs to be entered into to reduce the military budget by a large amount. If, beginning one year from now, we were to cut military spending by 25 percent from its projected levels, we would still be immeasurably stronger than any combination of nations with whom we might be engaged.

I am working with a variety of thoughtful analysts to show how we can make very substantial cuts in the military budget without in any way diminishing the security we need.

Implicitly, some advocates of continued largesse for the Pentagon concede that the case cannot be made fully in terms of our need to be safe from physical attack. Ironically—even hypocritically, since many of those who make the case are in other contexts anti-government spending conservatives—they argue for a kind of weaponized Keynesianism [economic agenda that encourages government spending to stimulate the economy] that says military spending is important because it provides jobs and boosts the economy. Spending on military hardware does produce some jobs, but it is one of the most inefficient ways to deploy public funds to stimulate the economy. When I asked him years ago what he thought about military spending as stimulus, [former head of the Federal Reserve] Alan Greenspan, to his credit, noted that from an economic standpoint military spending was like insurance: if necessary to meet its primary need, it had to be done, but it was not good for the economy; and to the extent that it could be reduced, the economy would benefit.

Military Spending Can Be Cut

The math is compelling: if we do not make reductions approximating 25 percent of the military budget starting fairly soon, it will be impossible to continue to fund an adequate level of domestic activity even with a repeal of Bush's tax cuts for the very wealthy.

I am working with a variety of thoughtful analysts to show how we can make very substantial cuts in the military budget without in any way diminishing the security we need. I do not think it will be hard to make it clear to Americans that their well-being is far more endangered by a proposal for substantial reductions in Medicare, Social Security, or other important domestic areas than it would be by canceling weapons systems that have no justification from any threat we are likely to face.

So those organizations, editorial boards, and individuals who talk about the need for fiscal responsibility should be challenged to begin with the area where our spending has been the most irresponsible and has produced the least good for the dollars expended—our military budget. Both parties have for too long indulged the implicit notion that military spending is somehow irrelevant to reducing the deficit and have resisted applying to military spending the standards of efficiency that are applied to other programs. If we do not reduce the military budget, either we accustom ourselves to unending and increasing budget deficits, or we do severe harm to our ability to improve the quality of our lives through sensible public policy.

13

There Is a Link Between Economic Decline and Diminished Military Strength

Loren Thompson

Loren Thompson is chief operating officer of the Lexington Institute, a libertarian think tank.

The strength of America's military has been a reflection of its economic strength. U.S. economic strength has been declining steadily during the past decade, however, and this decline is reflected in the current budget deficit, among other things. The deficit inevitably will affect military budgets and expenditures. The current defense program probably is unsustainable if America's economic decline continues. In the future, policy makers will need to look more closely at both the positive and the negative consequences of military spending and will need to think more carefully about the best ways to allocate military expenditures.

The U.S. has possessed the most powerful economy in the world for so long that no one can remember a time when America was not No. 1. The armed forces have been a big beneficiary of the nation's economic success. Although Pentagon planners frequently complain about having to operate in a "fiscally constrained" environment, the U.S. accounts for nearly half of global military outlays.

It is a remarkable reflection of America's economic strength that less than 5 percent of the world's population can sustain such a high level of defense spending, using less than 5 percent of gross domestic product.

But what if America ceased to be the world's biggest creditor, its largest producer of goods, its most successful trader? Sad to say, those questions are no longer hypothetical. Over the last 30 years, the nation that practically invented free enterprise has become the world's biggest debtor, has witnessed the rapid decline of a manufacturing sector once dubbed the "arsenal of democracy," and has accumulated an annual trade deficit equivalent to more than $2,000 per citizen per year.

In other words, America's economy is in decline. The problem isn't just a severe cyclical downturn caused by excesses in the housing market. The economy is undergoing a more profound, secular erosion that has resulted in it giving up a little more of its share of global output every year in this decade, in much the same way that General Motors and Ford have gradually yielded share in the domestic automobile market. When the current decade began, America generated nearly a third of world output. By the time it ends, America will claim barely a quarter. Optimists such as Fareed Zakaria describe this trend as "the rise of the rest," but it might just as easily be called the decline of the West, especially America.

The negative economic news has not yet had much impact on the thinking of military analysts. They are accustomed to thinking of defense as one of the few sectors in the national economy driven by noneconomic forces, namely threats and politics. But if the country's economy continues to weaken, it is inevitable that the resulting scarcity of funds will force reductions in military outlays. Furthermore, the decline of specific industrial sectors such as steelmaking, electronics, chemicals and pharmaceuticals will limit the options military planners have for sustaining the most demanding military campaigns. So policymakers need to take a hard look at what current economic trends mean for the nation's future military preparedness.

The place to start is by asking three basic questions. First, how serious is the decline in America's economic power? Second, what does the decline portend for the affordability of the planned defense program? And third, how can defense outlays be structured so that they help the economy rather than hurt it? Liberals and conservatives alike will question the wisdom of making defense spending decisions according to economic criteria, but as the following analysis indicates, separation of the two spheres is no longer affordable because Washington is out of money.

How Serious?

Shortly before President Barack Obama took office, the U.S. intelligence community's top analyst completed a major assessment of global trends through 2025. The analyst, Thomas Fingar, predicted that the international system would be "transformed" over the next 15 years in much the same way that it was remade after World War II. But unlike during the Cold War, when America rose to unrivaled supremacy, Fingar's study predicted it would be China that had the most influence on global politics and economics in the years ahead. The U.S. would probably remain the single most powerful nation in the near term, Fingar concluded, but in relative terms, China would be rising fast, and America would be declining.

Fingar traced the source of these trends mainly to America's loss of economic power. He said, "In terms of size, speed and directional flow, the transfer of global wealth and economic power now under way—roughly from West to East—is without precedent in modern history." Shortly after Fingar's findings became public, former Deputy Treasury Secretary Robert Altman rendered a similar verdict in *Foreign Affairs* keyed to the credit-market collapse. Altman warned that the unfolding financial crisis "is a major geopolitical setback for the United States and Europe," and predicted it would "accelerate trends that are shifting the world's center of gravity away from the United States." He too saw China as a rising power poised to capitalize on America's decline.

Such fears might be overstated in much the same way that warnings of Japan's rise were overdone a generation ago. Concern about national decline has been a commonplace topic among intellectuals since Edward Gibbon published the first volume of *The Decline and Fall of the Roman Empire* in 1776. Clearly, some of the more pessimistic predictions from past generations were wrong. Even today, there is much misinformation in the public media about precisely what's wrong with America. For example, as a recent Rand Corp. study pointed out, it is hard to argue that American science is in decline when the nation generates 40 percent of all research spending among industrialized countries, produces a similar share of patented innovations, and hosts three-quarters of the world's top 40 universities. In a typical year, IBM generates more technology patents than all of China combined.

However, America's scientific prowess is no longer translating into economic strength the way it once was. A review of economic trends over the past decade reveals rapid deterioration in the solvency and competitiveness of the U.S. economy.

Economic growth. The growth of the economy has lagged behind the rest of the world for a dozen years, averaging barely 2 percent annually during the Bush administration. From 2000 to 2008, the U.S. share of global output fell from 31 percent to 27 percent. While the U.S. endured twin recessions at the beginning and end of President George W. Bush's tenure—and anemic growth in between—China's growth rate averaged about 10 percent annually throughout the decade.

Family income. The modest expansion that followed the dot-com meltdown at the beginning of Bush's first term produced no income gain for average families, the first time that has ever happened. Median household income remained stuck at about $61,000 annually, even as the price of everything from housing to health care to energy went up. The CIA estimates that all of the gains in income in the U.S. since 1975 have gone to the upper 20 percent of households.

Job creation. The last eight years have witnessed the lowest rate of private-sector job creation on record since World War II. Most of the gains in employment have occurred in government or in areas closely related to government spending, such as education and health care. Meanwhile, the manufacturing sector has lost an average of 50,000 jobs every month for eight straight years.

Trade balance. The nation's annual trade deficit has doubled from an already sizable $380 billion at the beginning of the decade to well over $700 billion today. While much of the increase is traceable to rising oil prices that have fallen in recent months, the nation is also running a deficit of more than a billion dollars per day in manufactured goods. The imbalance has weakened the value of the dollar while leading to vast accumulations of U.S. currency in foreign hands.

Budget deficit. The debt of the federal government has nearly doubled from $5.7 trillion at the beginning of the decade to almost $11 trillion today. The yearly balance of federal outlays and tax receipts, which was substantially in surplus when President Bush entered office, deteriorated to a $480 billion deficit in fiscal 2008, and is expected to exceed a trillion dollars in fiscal 2009. Obama has warned of trillion-dollar deficits for years to come as a result of the current economic crisis.

Bad as these broad-based indicators sound, they do not capture the full extent of erosion in some parts of the economy relevant to military power. That is especially true of the manufacturing sector, which includes most of the so-called defense-industrial base. While aerospace companies are doing reasonably well, the overall health of U.S. manufacturing has been weakening for decades. The near collapse of the domestically owned auto industry is just the latest indication of decline. Commercial shipbuilding and consumer electronics industries have largely disappeared since the 1980s, while U.S. steelmakers now account for only 7 percent of global output (compared to 38 percent for Chinese steelmakers). Furthermore, the migration of manufacturing overseas is not confined to traditional metal-bending activities: the pharmaceutical industry is now incapable of manufacturing antibiotics such as penicillin without supplies from China.

In fiscal 2008, defense spending, broadly defined, claimed about 5 percent of gross domestic product and 23 percent of the federal budget. In addition to the baseline defense budget of $479 billion, $188 billion was spent on military operations in Iraq and Afghanistan, and $22 billion was spent on related activities outside the defense department, most notably the energy department's nuclear weapons program. The resulting total—$689 billion—is widely viewed as the peak level of military outlays in the current decade since spending in the baseline budget is programmed to stabilize in subsequent years and expenditures on overseas operations are expected to fall.

The most recent CBO estimate of the federal budget projects that in fiscal 2009, the government will spend the equivalent of 25 percent of gross domestic product while taking in 17 percent.

Although it is too early to calculate the claim that defense spending will make on the economy in 2009 given the ongoing contraction of commercial markets, military spending of all kinds is likely to total about $670 billion for the year—representing roughly twice the buying power of the Pentagon budget when the decade began. Proponents of robust military spending frequently argue that a defense commitment of that magnitude should be easily sustainable within a $14 trillion economy, especially given the likely decline in outlays for overseas operations. According to the Congressional Budget

Office (CBO), if current plans for the baseline budget remain on track, regular military spending would drop to 3.1 percent of gross domestic product in 2013 and 2.5 percent in 2026. The latter figure is well below the lowest level of economic commitment made to military activities during the Clinton years, now remembered as a period of depressed defense spending.

Unsustainable Deficit

So it is not hard to see why defense analysts haven't spent much time thinking about the affordability of the current defense plan. However, all of the projections of future military spending assume that the U.S. economy will continue growing at close to the historical average of about 3 percent annually. If that growth were to cease or reverse for a prolonged period of time, the resulting tensions within the federal budget would preclude steady funding of military activities unless there was a surge in threats. The most recent CBO estimate of the federal budget projects that in fiscal 2009, the government will spend the equivalent of 25 percent of gross domestic product while taking in 17 percent, resulting in the need to borrow more than a trillion dollars. A deficit of that scale is not sustainable over the long run, and even in the short run depends on the willingness of overseas lenders—who have bought four-fifths of Treasury debt in recent years—to continue lending despite weakness in their own economies.

Beyond the parlous state of federal finances, there are other reasons to doubt the affordability of the present defense plan. For example, CBO estimates that once unbudgeted costs are included in defense totals, military outlays will average $652 billion annually in constant 2009 dollars over the next 18 years. That is barely any decrease at all from the peak level of funding seen in the current decade when overseas contingencies and ancillary items are included. Yet the peak level of funding in this decade is well higher than the top end of the spending range seen over the previous 50 years, so it probably isn't sustainable given the many other obligations the federal government has taken on in that time.

If federal debt payments—now more than a billion dollars daily—and entitlement programs weren't growing rapidly, the current level of military outlays might be sustainable in normal economic circumstances. But once the reality of a declining economy is combined with unfunded entitlement obligations of $43 trillion, the funding of defense needs looks doubtful. Entitlement programs are treated as formula-driven "mandatory" obligations within the federal budget, which means they are structurally and politically harder to restrain than the "discretionary" outlays in the defense budget. And even within the discretionary categories of federal outlays (about 45 percent of the total budget), defense must compete with such politically popular activities as the environment, education, criminal justice, and general science.

The erosion of national economic power will be paced by the erosion of national military power.

As if all this were not enough, the parts of the defense program that are politically easiest to cut—the investment accounts—are the parts that contribute most tangibly to long-term military power. If military pay and benefits are slashed, the consequences are felt quickly in the field and on Capitol Hill. The same is true if readiness accounts are cut. With military health care costs having risen 144 percent during the present decade, there are compelling reasons to try to restrain their further growth (one Pentagon panel called cost increases in military health care an "existential threat" to the future defense posture). But investment in the future is almost always easier to cut than current consumption, because the near-term consequences in the field are imperceptible, and the domestic impact is felt in only a handful of congressional districts.

The bottom line, then, is that the current defense program will probably not be sustainable if the decline of the economy continues, and when the cutting begins to bring military outlays into closer alignment with available resources, the first items to go will be those that contribute most to the nation's long-term military power. In other words, the erosion of national economic power will be paced by the erosion of national military power.

A Drain or a Boost?

Military spending traditionally has been viewed as a drain on the economy, which was one reason the government seldom spent more than 1 percent of gross domestic product on defense in peacetime before 1950. That pattern changed during the Cold War, when sustained high levels of military expenditure made the "military-industrial complex" a seemingly permanent fixture on the economic landscape. Weapons research during that period is now widely credited with boosting the development of key industries such as computers and semiconductors. When the Cold War ended, though, the Clinton administration slashed military research. The Bush administration restored funding without giving serious consideration to the connection between defense spending and economic growth.

Today, the connection needs to be examined more closely because the economy is in decline and the government is running out of money. Policymakers no longer have the luxury of spending a fifth of the federal budget on national defense without considering how those expenditures might help or hurt the economy. Relatively little research has been done on the subject, and much of it is tendentious. But even a cursory review of the data suggests that military activities have positive and negative economic consequences. For example, the exceedingly complex weapons acquisition system probably harms the competitiveness of military suppliers by impeding efficiency; on the other hand, weapons development also sustains hundreds of thousands of scientists and engineers who potentially contribute to the nation's economic growth. Similarly, military recruiting activities may bid up the price of scarce labor by offering pay and benefits superior to what private-sector employers can afford, but the military also provides millions of personnel with training that proves useful when they return to the mainstream economy.

So military spending has mixed economic results, some of them positive and some of them negative. It is not a good way of quickly stimulating the economy because its effects are indirect, and money appropriated for weapons typically takes years to be spent. But compared with other ways of putting money into the hands of consumers, it definitely has some desirable effects. For instance, much of the money taxpayers receive as a result of tax cuts may end up being spent on consumer durables from overseas such as automobiles, producing little net stimulus to the economy, whereas the vast preponderance of military outlays are spent in America on domestic goods and services. It may not make much sense to buy weapons simply to stimulate economic activity, but if there is a valid military requirement for equipment, then the case for its purchase is bolstered by its additional economic benefits.

Looking beyond the immediate economic crisis spawned by speculative activity in the housing market, the way in which military budgets are allocated may have an important impact on the more profound, secular decline that the economy is facing, which is largely traceable to the erosion of the manufacturing base. If system specifications are modified to minimize military-unique features and barriers to merging military workloads with commercial workloads are dismantled, then the economic benefits of defense investment outlays can be increased even though weapons outlays are falling. There would also be real economic advantages to thinking through where defense research and procurement funding is concentrated, both in terms of localities and technologies. These issues need to be considered much more rigorously today than in the past, because America's future as a global economic and military power can no longer be taken for granted.

14

Retirement of Baby Boomers Threatens to Create Unmanageable Deficits

Peter J. Nelson

Peter J. Nelson is a policy fellow at the Center of the American Experiment, a nonpartisan pubic policy institution.

As the first baby boomers, born in the middle of the twentieth century, enter retirement the country is facing a crisis of entitlement spending, coupled with rising health-care costs, which will lead to unmanageable budget deficits. Entitlement programs— Medicare, Medicaid, and Social Security—must be taken off "autopilot," and sustainable budgets for these program must be enacted and regularly reviewed. The costs need to be transparent within the overall budget so that entitlement spending can be considered along with other spending priorities.

Twelve years ago [1996], Peter G. Peterson—secretary of commerce under President Richard Nixon, former chairman of Lehman Brothers, cofounder of the Concord Coalition and longtime crusader for fiscal responsibility—wrote a book that asked, "Will America grow up before it grows old?"

Peterson was speaking about whether the United States would ever confront the budget mess and intergenerational clash certain to occur when baby boomers [the generation born during the middle of the 20th century] begin retiring in larger numbers. Medicare, Medicaid, and Social Security budgets were never equipped to handle this mass of retirees.

Looming Retirements Create Alarm

Today, as the first baby boomers enter retirement, there's little evidence America has grown up.

In fact, last month [July 2008] Congress again moved to duck the issue.

The Medicare Modernization Act of 2003 established a "Medicare funding warning" that Medicare trustees must clang when Medicare becomes over-reliant on general revenues. Such a warning triggers a requirement that the president must recommend ways of reducing reliance on general revenues, and Congress must then consider those recommendations on an expedited basis.

Last year [2007] the Medicare trustees did sound an alarm. President [George W.] Bush dutifully made his recommendations, and Congress had until July 30 this year to act on them, but instead they changed the rules and delayed action for another year.

The truth is, the 2003 legislation creating the warning system was itself a cop-out. It implied that it's OK to wait, that Medicare's fiscal solvency will only be in real trouble when the warning gets triggered. But it's not OK. Waiting shifted more debt to younger generations and aggravated the inevitable pain we'll feel when we make the hard choices necessary to bring our fiscal future into balance.

Both Parties Are to Blame

While Democrats can be blamed for the rule change in the House, the Medicare Modernization Act represents a truly bipartisan evasion.

Frustration with this bipartisan foot-dragging is fostering some unlikely alliances. Recently, the Brookings Institution on the left and the Heritage Foundation on the right brought together an ideologically diverse group of budget policy experts to address what they call "the huge problem the candidates are not talking about."

The result was a joint report, "Taking Back Our Fiscal Future."

While this group of policy experts disagree (and often quite sharply) on specific policy solutions, they do agree on the severity of the problem. Most importantly, they agree on a starting point.

The problem: Rapid growth in entitlement spending due to retiring baby boomers, coupled with rising health care costs, will lead to unmanageable budget deficits; a need to raise taxes at the expense of economic growth, and/or the inability to meet other vital priorities, particularly investments in younger populations.

While . . . policy experts disagree (and often quite sharply) on specific policy solutions, they do agree on the severity of the problem.

Autopilot Spending Must End

To avoid this fiscal mess, the group agreed that we should "take the three major entitlement programs off autopilot." By autopilot, it's referring to the fact that spending on entitlements takes place outside the normal budget process and automatically increases based on the number of people eligible. Consequently, entitlement budgets rarely get reviewed, and Congress and the president are never forced to balance entitlement spending with other priorities such as national defense, transportation, and education.

To shut off autopilot spending, the group made the following recommendations:

- Enact sustainable long-term budgets for the big three entitlements that set limits on automatic spending growth with a review required every five years.

- Establish a trigger that forces specific actions when a five-year review predicts that spending will outpace the budget. These actions might include automatic benefit reductions, premium increases, tax increases, or specific action by Congress.

- Make the long-run costs of the three entitlements transparent within the overall budget so that entitlement spending is considered alongside other spending priorities.

America's fiscal train is not waiting for more baby boomers to retire before it wrecks.

A Train Wreck Waiting to Happen

Critics complain that the recommendations neglect specific issues driving up budget deficits, such as health-care costs and President Bush's tax cuts. But these are the sort of wedge issues the group wisely took pains to avoid. Instead, the group hopes to "set in motion a process that will yield an outcome that ultimately only the people and their representatives can craft."

America's fiscal train is not waiting for more baby boomers to retire before it wrecks. The White House predicts that next year's budget deficit will explode to a record $482 billion.

While modernizing America's entitlement programs will no doubt be contentious, the recommendations just outlined create a space where political leaders can show some maturity and begin the process.

Organizations to Contact

The editors have compiled the following list of organizations concerned with the issues debated in this book. The descriptions are derived from materials provided by the organizations. All have publications or information available for interested readers. The list was compiled on the date of publication of the present volume; the information provided here may change. Readers need to remember that many organizations take several weeks or longer to respond to inquiries.

The Brookings Institution

1775 Massachusetts Ave. NW, Washington, DC 20036
(202) 797-6000
Web site: www.brookings.edu

The institution, founded in 1927, is a liberal think tank that conducts research and education on foreign policy, economics, government, and the social sciences. Among many other publications, it publishes the quarterly *Brookings Review* and the biannual *Brookings Papers on Economic Activity*.

The Cato Institute

1000 Massachusetts Ave. NW, Washington, DC 20036
(202) 842-0200
Web site: www.cato.org

The Cato Institute is a nonprofit public policy research organization. Its mission is to increase the understanding of public policies based on the principles of limited government, free markets, individual liberty, and peace. The organization publishes numerous newsletters, journals, and reviews, including the *Tax & Budget Bulletin*.

Center on Budget and Policy Priorities
820 First St. NE, Suite 510, Washington, DC   20002
(202) 408-1080
Web site: www.cbpp.org

The Center on Budget and Policy Priorities is a nonprofit research organization that focuses on how budgetary policy impacts low- and moderate-income Americans. Resources produced by the center address a wide variety of issues, including the budget process, deficits and projections, children's health insurance and nutrition, welfare reform, and the tax code.

Center for Economic and Policy Research (CEPR)
1611 Connecticut Ave. NW, Suite 400, Washington, DC   20009
(202) 293-5380
Web site: www.cepr.net

The Center for Economic and Policy Research conducts professional research and public education programs to promote democratic debate about important economic and social issues. CEPR is committed to presenting issues in an accurate and understandable manner, so that the public is better prepared to choose among the various policy options. CEPR asserts that an informed public should be able to choose policies that lead to an improving quality of life, both for people within the United States and around the world.

Committee on the Budget, U.S. House of Representatives
207 Cannon House Office Bldg.
Washington, DC   20515-6065
(202) 226-7200
Web site: http://budget.house.gov

According to the Rules of the House of Representatives, the House Budget Committee is responsible for "establishment, extension, and enforcement of special controls over the Federal budget, including the budgetary treatment of off-budget Federal agencies." The Web site includes answers to frequently asked questions about the budget process, laws governing the budgeting process, and current budget statistics.

The Concord Coalition

1011 Arlington Blvd., Suite 300, Arlington, VA   22209
(703) 894-6222
Web site: www.concordcoalition.org

The Concord Coalition is a nonpartisan grassroots organization that seeks to educate the public about the causes and consequences of deficit spending on the part of the federal government. Subjects covered include the national debt, the federal budget, Medicare and health care, social security, and tax entitlements.

The Congressional Budget Office (CBO)

Ford House Office Bldg., 4th Floor
Washington, DC   20515-6925
(202) 226-2600
Web site: www.cbo.gov

The Congressional Budget Office's mandate is to provide objective and timely analysis of budget proposals to the House and Senate budget committees and members of the legislature and to support the legislative process. The CBO Web site posts analyses of the economic impact of virtually every spending proposal considered by Congress. Recent publications address the long-term budget outlook, the impact of health insurance policy on labor markets, and the economic costs of taxing carbon dioxide emissions.

Demos

220 Fifth Ave., 5th Floor, New York, NY   10001
(212) 633-1405
Web site: www.demos.org

Demos is a nonpartisan public policy research and advocacy organization that works with advocates and policy makers around the country in pursuit of four overarching goals: (1) a more equitable economy with widely shared prosperity and opportunity; (2) a vibrant and inclusive democracy with high levels of voting and civic engagement; (3) an empowered public sector that works for the common good; and (4) responsible U.S. engagement in an interdependent world.

The Heritage Foundation

214 Massachusetts Ave. NE, Washington, DC   20002-4999
(202) 546-4400
Web site: www.heritage.org

The Heritage Foundation is a research and educational institute whose mission is to formulate and promote conservative public policies based on the principles of free enterprise, limited government, individual freedom, traditional American values, and a strong national defense. The organization's Web site features newsletters and blogs as well as offering for sale print publications on various topics.

Public Agenda

6 E. Thirty-ninth St., 9th Floor, New York, NY   10016
(212) 686-6610
Web site: www.publicagenda.org

Public Agenda is a nonpartisan, nonprofit public policy research and education organization that seeks to bridge the gap between American leaders and what the public really thinks about issues ranging from education to foreign policy to immigration to religion and civility in American life. It pursues its mission by helping American leaders better understand the public's point of view and by helping citizens know more about critical policy issues so they can make thoughtful, informed decisions.

Senate Budget Committee

624 Dirksen Senate Office Bldg., Washington, DC   20510
(202) 224-0642
Web site: http://budget.senate.gov

Along with the House Budget Committee, the Senate Budget Committee is responsible for drafting Congress's annual budget plan and monitoring action on the budget for the federal government. The Budget Committee's Web site links to separate resources on the budget posted by Senate Republicans and Senate Democrats.

Bibliography

Books

Ari Aisen and David Hauner — *Budget Deficits and Interest Rates: A Fresh Perspective.* Washington, DC: International Monetary Fund, 2008.

Alan J. Auerbach — *Federal Budget Rules: The U.S. Experience.* Cambridge, MA: National Bureau of Economic Research, 2008.

Bruce R. Bartlett — *Imposter: How George W. Bush Bankrupted America and Betrayed the Reagan Legacy.* New York: Doubleday, 2006.

Fred C. Bergsten — *The Long-Term International Economic Position of the United States.* Washington DC: Peterson Institute for International Economics, 2009.

Scott Bittle and Jean Johnson — *Where Does the Money Go? Your Guided Tour to the Federal Budget Crisis.* New York: Collins, 2008.

Brian Cashell — *The Economics of the Federal Budget Deficit.* Washington, DC: Congressional Research Service, Library of Congress, 2005.

William Russell Easterly — *Walking Up the Down Escalator: Public Investment and Fiscal Stability.* Washington, DC: World Bank Development Research Group, 2007.

Chris Edwards   *Downsizing the Federal Government.* Washington, DC: Cato Institute, 2005.

Jasmine Farrier   *Passing the Buck: Congress, the Budget and Deficits.* Lexington: University Press of Kentucky, 2004.

Ellen Frank   *The Raw Deal: How Myths and Misinformation About Deficits, Inflation and Wealth Impoverish America.* Boston: Beacon, 2004.

James K. Galbraith   *The Predator State: How Conservatives Abandoned the Free Market and Why Liberals Should Too.* New York: Free Press, 2008.

Marc J. Hetherington   *Why Trust Matters: Declining Political Trust and the Demise of American Liberalism.* Princeton, NJ: Princeton University Press, 2005.

David Johnston   *Free Lunch: How the Wealthiest Americans Enrich Themselves at Your Expense (and Stick You with the Bill).* New York: Portfolio, 2007.

Robert E. Kelly   *The National Debt of the United States, 1941–2008.* Jefferson, NC: McFarland, 2008.

Donald F. Kettl   *Deficit Politics: The Search for Balance in American Politics.* New York: Longman, 2003.

Valentino Larcinese, Riccardo Puglisi, and James M. Snyder	*Partisan Bias in Economic News: Evidence on the Agenda-Setting Behavior of U.S. Newspapers.* Cambridge, MA: National Bureau of Economic Research, 2007.
Michael Leeds, Peter Von Allmen, and Richard Shiming	*Macroeconomics.* Boston: Pearson Addison-Wesley, 2006.
James B. Lucas	*National Deficit and Debt: Where to Next?* New York: Nova Books, 2005.
Julia Lynch	*Age in the Welfare State: The Origins of Social Spending on Pensioners, Workers and Children.* New York: Cambridge University Press, 2006.
Grover Glenn Norquist	*Leave Us Alone: Getting the Government's Hands Off Our Money, Our Guns, Our Lives.* New York: Morrow, 2008.
Peter M. Peterson	*Running on Empty: How the Democratic and Republican Parties Are Bankrupting Our Future and What Americans Can Do About It.* Prince Frederick, MD: RB, 2005.
Alice M. Rivlin and Isabel V. Sawhill	*Restoring Fiscal Sanity, 2005: Meeting the Long-Run Challenge.* Washington, DC: Brookings Institution Press, 2005.

Christina Romer | *The Macroeconomic Effects of Tax Changes: Estimates Based on a New Measure of Fiscal Shocks.* Cambridge, MA: National Bureau of Economic Research, 2007.

Allen Schick | *The Federal Budget: Politics, Policy, Process.* Washington, DC: Brookings Institution Press, 2007.

Daniel N. Shaviro | *Taxes, Spending and the U.S. Government's March Toward Bankruptcy.* New York: Cambridge University Press, 2007.

Joel Slemrod and Jon M. Bakja | *Taxing Ourselves: A Citizen's Guide to the Debate over Taxes.* Cambridge, MA, MIT Press, 2008.

Joseph E. Stiglitz and Aaron Edlin | *The Economists' Voice: Top Economists Take on Today's Problems.* New York: Columbia University Press, 2008.

M.L. Walden | *Smart Economics: Commonsense Answers to 50 Questions about Government, Taxes, Business, and Households.* Westport, CT: Praeger, 2005.

Addison Wiggin, Kate Incontrera, and Dorianne Perrucci | *I.O.U.S.A.* Hoboken, NJ: Wiley, 2008.

Robert E. Wright | *One Nation Under Debt: Hamilton, Jefferson, and the History of What We Owe.* New York: McGraw-Hill, 2008.

Periodicals

Roger C. Altman "We'll Need to Raise Taxes Soon: Expect Congress to Seriously Consider a Value-Added Tax," *Wall Street Journal*, June 30, 2009.

Edmund L. Andrews "A Crisis Trumps Constraint," *Investor's Business Daily*, January 1, 2009.

Alan J. Auerbach and William G. Gale "Here Comes the Next Fiscal Crisis: Without Action by Policymakers, an Increasing Imbalance Between Federal Spending and Revenues Will Produce a Dangerous Deficit," *Los Angeles Times*, July 8, 2009.

Baltimore Sun "Republican Bruce Bartlett: We Must Raise Taxes," (interview), July 17, 2009.

Matthew Benjamin "Democrats Split on Stimulus as Job Losses Mount, Deficit Soars," Bloomberg.com, July 25, 2009. www.bloomberg.com.

Carl M. Cannon "Is It Obama's Economy Yet?" *Politics Daily*, June 29, 2009.

Andrew Cassel "Where Have We Heard This Warning Before?" *Philadelphia Inquirer*, January 19, 2007.

Chicago Tribune "Obama Aims to Cut Federal Budget Deficit in Half: Ending Iraq War and Raising Taxes on Wealthy Are Keys," February 22, 2009.

CQ Weekly "Fiscal '09 Deficit of $1.2 Trillion in CBO Estimate," January 12, 2009.

Thomas R. Eddlem "Obama Sells $1 Trillion Health Care Spending Increase as Deficit Control," *New American*, July 23, 2009.

Peter S. Goodman "Staggering Budget Gap and a Reluctance to Fill It," *New York Times*, July 7, 2009.

Jennifer Haberkorn "Savings Seen in Cutting Health Care Growth," *Washington Times*, June 2, 2009.

Jocelyn Hanamirian "The Green Miles," *Conde Nast Portfolio*, March 2009.

Patrice Hill "Summers: Switch from Spending to Producing to Fix Economy," *Washington Times*, July 18, 2009.

Houston Chronicle "Red Ink Rises as Deficit Nears $1 Trillion," June 11, 2009.

Raymond Keating "In D.C., Wasteful Spending Is the Name of the Game," *Long Island Business News*, August 15, 2008.

Lewiston (ID) Morning Tribune "Obama Inherits Bush's Deficits Plus Blame," June 20, 2009.

Manufacturing & Technology News "Federal Budget Deficit Zooms off the Map," September 15, 2008.

William McKenzie "Why the Federal Debt Should Worry Us," *Dallas Morning News*, July 13, 2009.

William Milberg   "Is the Sky Falling? Questioning the Conventional Wisdom on the U.S. Trade and Budget Deficits," *Challenge*, December 2007.

Frank Newport   "Obama Rated Highest as Person, Lowest on Deficit, Spending," *Gallup Poll Briefing*, June 8, 2009.

Newsday   "U.S. Must Face Up to Dollar's Drop: Eliminate the Federal Budget Deficit," January 4, 2007.

Roanoke (VA) Times   "Reality Check on the Deficit: Sen. McCain Promises to Eliminate the Federal Budget Deficit in His First Term. He Just Leaves Out One Small Detail: How," July 16, 2008.

John L. Scherer   "Debt and Deficit," *USA Today*, May 2008.

Gerald F. Seib   "Seeking Gold in a Barrel of Red Ink," *Wall Street Journal*, May 8, 2009.

Gerald F. Seib   "White House Sends Signals on Deficit," *Wall Street Journal*, June 12, 2009.

Mike Soraghan   "'Pay-Go' Returns as Public Worries About Spending," *Hill*, July 20, 2009.

Newark (NJ) Star-Ledger   "F-22 Raptors: Shoot Down Wasteful Defense Spending," July 17, 2009.

John Stossel	"What's with All This 'Don't Worry About the Deficit' Talk?" *Fort Worth (TX)Business Press*, December 15, 2008.
Martin A. Sullivan	"The National Credit Card," *Tax Notes*, March 2, 2009.
USA Today	"Bernanke: U.S. Deficit Poses Risk to Fiscal Stability," June 4, 2009.
USA Today	"IRS Revenue Suffers in Economy," May 27, 2009.
Western Farm Press	"Budget Analysts Say U.S. Must 'Wake Up' to Fiscal Realities," February 21, 2009.
Armstrong Williams	"Senseless Stimulus Is Not Needed," *Spero News*, February 23, 2009. www.speroforum.com.

Index